HINTERLAND

Hinterland offers an answ[er] [to the]
question 'what is creative [writing]
by showcasing the best ne[w work in]
the fields of memoir, essay, travel and
food writing, reportage, psychoscape,
biography, flash non-fiction and more.

Our pages bring together work by
established, award-winning authors
alongside new writers, many of whom
we are thrilled to publish for the first time
and whose work, we promise, will merit
your full attention.

Often, the pieces you'll find in Hinterland
will straddle the boundaries between
strands and be difficult to classify:
we see this as a strength. Hinterland
intends to challenge, move, entertain
and, above all, be a fantastic read.

WELCOME TO ISSUE 9

Advocates for Hinterland:
Nathan Hamilton, Kathryn Hughes,
Helen Smith, Rebecca Stott, Ian Thomson

Editorial Team
Editors-In-Chief – Yin F. Lim & Andrew Kenrick
Art Direction & Design – Tom Hutchings
Business Support – Ben Watkins
Proofreaders – Susan K. Burton, Margaret Hedderman, Stephen Massil,
　　　　　　 Florence Pearce-Higginson, Claire Reiderman
　　　　　　 and Isabel Williams

Submissions
Hinterland is committed to paying writers and artists for all work we publish.
Please send us your work via Submittable:
hinterlandnonfiction.submittable.com
We accept submissions year-round and endeavour to reply within 4 months.
We regret we are unable to provide feedback.
There is a small fee of £3 per submission.

Subscriptions
An annual subscription to Hinterland (four issues, print and digital)
costs £40 U.K., £44 Europe, £54 Rest-of-world.
Digital subscription only, £20.
Please visit our website for full details.

Distribution
Hinterland is distributed worldwide by NBN International.
For all trade orders contact +44 (0) 1752 202301
orders@nbninternational.com

Advertising
Please see our website for current rates, or to discuss sponsorship please
contact us at hinterlandnonfiction@gmail.com

Acknowledgments
The Editors gratefully acknowledge financial contributions from
the UEA Publishing Project.

Find Hinterland online at
www.hinterlandnonfiction.com
or contact us: hinterlandnonfiction@gmail.com

ISBN: 978-1-913861-37-7
ISSN (Print): 2632-136X
ISSN (Online): 2632-1378

HINTERLAND

THE BEST NEW CREATIVE NON-FICTION

Issue 9
2021

Issue 9

NON-FICTION

Contributors

Jenn Ashworth's *(Robinson Daniel Jennifer Crusoe)* first novel, *A Kind of Intimacy*, was published in 2009 and won a Betty Trask Award. On the publication of her second, *Cold Light*, she was featured on the BBC's *The Culture Show* as one of the UK's twelve best new writers. In 2019 she published a memoir-in-essays, *Notes Made While Falling* which was a New Statesman Book of the Year and was shortlisted for the Gordon Burn Prize. Her latest novel is *Ghosted: A Love Story*. She lives in Lancashire and is a Professor of Writing at Lancaster University.

Aaron Landsman's *(Wrestling the Keys)* upcoming and recent publication credits include poetry in *The Wax Paper*, *Ghost City Review* and *Evergreen Review*, and prose in *River Teeth*, *Theater Magazine*, *Painted Bride Quarterly*, and *Hobart*. His new book about democracy and performance called *The City We Make Together*, co-authored with Mallory Catlett, comes out with the University of Iowa Press in 2022. His live performance works have been seen on stages, in homes, on buses and in offices, in New York City where he lives, and in other US and foreign cities. He teaches part-time at Princeton.

Chris Beckett *(Abebe, the Cook's Son)* is a Ted Hughes Award-shortlisted poet and translator who grew up in Addis Ababa in the last years of Haile Selassie's reign. He has published two collections, *Ethiopia Boy* and *Tenderfoot*, plus the first ever anthology of Ethiopian Amharic poetry in English, edited/translated with Alemu Tebeje, *Songs We Learn from Trees*. This autumn he is leading a workshop on Childhood and Praise Poetry for the Poetry School.

Jacqueline Ellis *(Zero Hour for the Rabbit)* is a writer and professor of women's and gender studies. Her writing has appeared in *Feminist Review*, *WSQ*, and *Mutha Magazine*. Originally from Peterborough, England, she now lives in Montclair, New Jersey.

Chris Cusack *(Birds)* is a writer and academic from the Netherlands. His work has appeared in *Poetry Ireland Review*, *The Manchester Review*, *Banshee*, *Ink Sweat & Tears*, *3:AM*, *The Honest Ulsterman*, and elsewhere. As a critic, he has written for the *TLS*, *The Irish Times*, *Poetry London* and *Poetry Review*.

Pune Dracker *(Gator Love)* is a writer, editor and social justice warrior in New York City. She has an MFA in Nonfiction/Poetry from The New School, where she conducted psychogeographic experiments and wrote and performed Fluxus-inspired scores, and an MA in Design Research, Writing & Criticism from the School of Visual Arts.

Doireann Ní Ghríofa *(In Conversation with…)* is a poet and essayist. Her prose début *A Ghost in the Throat* was awarded the James Tait Black Prize for Biography 2021 and described as 'powerful' (*New York Times*), and 'captivatingly original' (*The Guardian*). She is also author of six critically acclaimed books of poetry, each a deepening exploration of birth, death, desire, and domesticity. Awards for her writing include a Lannan Literary Fellowship (USA), the Ostana Prize (Italy), a Seamus Heaney Fellowship (Queen's University), and the Rooney Prize for Irish Literature.

Jordan Harrison-Twist's *(My Stepfather, Bolton's Entire First Eleven at the '95 Play-Off Final Against Reading)* most recent writings have appeared in *Ossian, The Cormorant Broadsheet, Lit Quarterly, CHEAP POP, No Contact, Funicular, Reflex Fiction, Lunate*, and others. He won the Retreat West micro fiction competition with his story 'Longitudinal', which was nominated for a Pushcart Prize. His forthcoming chapbook *A Few Alterations* will be published by Nightjar.

Tom Hutchings is our in-house Graphic Designer, and is still probably too excited by taking photos of the sky. You can see a selection of his work (including plenty of sky) on thorngraphicdesign.com

Alice Kent's *(Something Happened)* first short story 'Len's Whole Life' was selected for the Words and Women anthology. She was longlisted for the Grazia Bailey's Fiction First Chapter Award. Alice wrote the foreword for the pamphlet *Walking Norwich: The Real and Imagined City*, which featured in *The Guardian* and on BBC Radio 4's *Open Book*. She co-edited the 2021 pamphlet *Dialogues*, which includes Vahni Capildeo on Julian of Norwich and Valur Gunnarsson on W.G. (Max) Sebald. Alice studied Politics at the University of Birmingham and has a Masters in European Journalism having studied in Aarhus and Utrecht. She works at the social innovation foundation, Nesta, and lives in Norwich with her partner, two kids and cat, Mishka.

Laura Knott *(Screw You, Descartes)* studied environmental art and film/video at MIT, and political science and dance at Duke University. Her work has been published in the *Boston Art Review* and *Duke Magazine*, and by the MIT School of Architecture + Planning and the MIT Museum. Laura has edited a volume on Sky Art, curated exhibitions, produced a live-streamed work in which dancers danced simultaneously in 11 countries, and performed at the documenta exhibition. Her videos have appeared in Mexico, Greece, and the United States. A native of Mississippi, Laura grows food in her garden in Massachusetts, where she lives.

Carla Montemayor *(The Shapeshifters)* is originally from the Philippines and came to the UK as a student nearly 20 years ago. She has worked in politics and communication in three countries for most of her career, most recently in migrants' and women's rights. She was shortlisted for Spread the Word's Life Writing Prize in 2020 and is a recipient of the London Writers Awards 2021. She is working on a memoir on grief, family history and her life as a migrant in London over the turbulent decade.

Jon Paul Roberts *(In Search of Lost Voices)* is an essayist and cultural critic from the north of England. Their work has appeared in *The Spool, Another North, Brightest Young Things, Metro, The Huffington Post*, and elsewhere. Their bi-monthly column, 'How Film Changed Me', uses film and television to understand millennial life and is published by Big Picture Film Club. In 2017, they won the Spread the Word's inaugural Life Writing Prize for their essay '1955-2012'. Currently, they are working on a non-fiction book that grew out of 'In Search for Lost Voices' as well as finishing their PhD at Liverpool John Moores University.

Liz Taunt (*RUNE*) is our cover artist. She uses many different printmaking techniques including drypoint, lino, collagraph and monoprint, and she has recently been making collages from discarded prints. She is not interested in narrative or realism in her art, instead she is trying to bring something new into the world that combines the chaotic, the arbitrary and the awkward: things that surprise her and prompt the question 'where did that come from?' She gets lost (in a nice way) in a parallel world, and tries to invent ciphers and shorthand to describe her particular reality.

Editorial

Something we've noticed with both our recent submissions and many of the books on our to-read pile is that writers of creative non-fiction have never been more playful with form. Hence, this issue celebrates the art of experimentation.

What's striking about the work featured in Issue 9 are the diverse paths taken in the storytelling. In her epistle to the author of a childhood book, Jenn Ashworth reflects on how our reading forms us. Poetry is the basis of Chris Beckett's remembrance of his first love in 1960s Ethiopia, and also of Alice Kent's literary dance through the sciences and the arts. Carla Montemayor breathes new life onto old lore as she explores her family's storytelling heritage. And whether it's Laura Knott's fragmentary dissection of her parents' minds, Jordan Harrison-Twist's use of a football club's first-eleven to frame his stepfather-stepson narrative or Pune Dracker's playful riff on an urban legend, each piece defies definition and boundaries.

Yin F Lim spent many years as a journalist writing other people's stories before deciding to write her own. She completed a Creative Non-Fiction MA at the University of East Anglia and now mainly writes about family, food and migration.

Issue 9 also features quietly moving pieces, from Jacqueline Ellis' ambivalent relationship with nature to Jon Paul Roberts' search for their late grandmother's voice. Aaron Landsman grapples with climate-change anxieties in the US while Chris Cusack scours the Dutch countryside for birds and language.

Last but not least, we have a conversation with Doireann Ní Ghríofa about her fascination with form and how she's reclaiming erased voices with her genre-defying book *A Ghost in the Throat*.

We hope you enjoy these exquisitely crafted works as much as we have.

The Editors

Andrew Kenrick has worked as an archaeologist and an archivist, a writer and an editor. He is currently studying for a PhD at the University of East Anglia, where he also teaches English Literature and Publishing.

Wrestling the Keys

by Aaron Landsman

First, you want to avoid any cliché talk of bounty;
of a simple quotidian life, just being attentive and
sensitive, just recognizing, you know, how lucky you
are – blessed, really – to be here on the planet, to
be loved, etc. Blessed with the people in your circle,
and even more just the simple things like pavement
smells, iron or wood smells, the fragrances of the
city, all of them intense, satisfying, redolent, even,
even if difficult?

You want to avoid the cliché of simple gratitude
for the small wonder of living, so before your son
wakes up on this particular Sunday you pay more
attention to the news. You think structurally and
get strategic. Because you also try to avoid the
dystopian clichés that already occupy too much of
your time: rescue from rooftops, neighbors helping
neighbors in another losing game of rising, unclean
water, or no water left at all; fire aglow across the
whole horizon; huddling near the one working air-
conditioner in the apartment down the hall, which
you all pool money to run, when the temperature
climbs, when the electricity even works.

You want to avoid those, too, so before your son
wakes up you think about plans. Should you buy
land upstate, fix up the apartment, move back to
the Midwest before prices go up in fill-in-the-blank-
more-habitable-city further inland?

Does avoiding doom have to mean succumbing to simplistic happiness? Is all happiness actually simplistic, which you've wondered at least since *Anna Karenina*, though that sullen and clichéd supposition is also something you've tried to avoid, but it keeps coming back?

What thwarts your valiant attempt to hold yourself productively within this charged tensegrity – between disaster and hollow gratitude with any kind of urbane remove – is when your son wakes up and you go together to the farmers' market, like most Sundays.

The market is on the corner of the park where junkies play chess next to their shaggy backpacks, their forlorn dogs, in between bouts of mania and lethargy. You thank your lucky location-location-location every week when you come here; who on a budget like yours gets a place a block away from a farmers' market in Manhattan?

Together, you and your son hold your noses walking by the compost station. You avoid the young white guy with easy hair and too much verve selling green energy. Each week you pass him and silently register your suspicion of market solutions to apocalypse.

Each week you pick out a selection of apples, based on how last week's tasted, and on the names: Pink Lady; NY429; Arlet; one more sweet-tart, one more crisp, one more round, more red.

Next you haggle with each other over which sweet bakery treat at the next booth you will share on the way home. The pecan sticky bun always wins.

A couple more booths down, you chat with Paul, the fish guy, whose knowledge of different species' mouth shapes and fin placements is legendary at your house. Paul and your son talk about bass and bluefish and mackerel. Paul could be your father in a different life. If your father had not been an activist lawyer and professor, he'd have been a fish guy, you're sure of it, and every day you would think and possibly write relatively simplistic, short, happy tomes, kind of like this one; paeans to the deep wisdom of the old Jewish fish guy on Avenue A, who is or could be or was your father. You would call up or imagine an ancestry for the whole planet, water and land, shtetls and seders, vaudeville and tenements.

The next stall is the meat guy, and he always seems burdened by the farm where he raises animals and eggs. You try to cheer him up by saying *the fried chicken we made last week turned out great.* He stares in a blank and almost hostile way before he ducks to the curb and takes a furtive hit off his vaping device.

Thanks.

You wonder if he's preoccupied by calculating: how many wings are unsold, how much is gas money back upstate, how late will the first frost hit? Your son brags again about your fried chicken. You worry it might be unbecoming to weep right now, at his naïve pride in your kitchen skills. That kind of quotidian joy, etc.

You calculate: your son is nine; when will his bubble burst? When did yours toward your actual father? When did his toward you?

You get carrots and potatoes at the next stall, then start home holding hands, holding your nose again by the compost, again dodging the green energy guy.

Your son whispers, *Every week, he literally asks: 'Are you interested in going green today?'*

Every week you hear the guy and you think to yourself: *it's 75 degrees in October, man.* It's too late to go green.

You are thinking about how, during hurricane Sandy, the water on Avenue C was four feet deep, while Avenue B just had a couple inches, and how do we measure progress since then?

You are trying to fit getting arrested into your schedule because you want this boy – this tagging and dancing boy, sparring with you now on Avenue B, waiting for the traffic light to change, at nine just too old to be fooled by the trick you used to do to seem like you could change the light by your own magic – *hocus pocus dominocus, magic light turn green* – you want him to know how much you would do to make his future more possible. On a more cynical day you just hope he will forgive you when you are gone, and he is without you amidst the flooding or burning.

Once, a few months ago, in a rush to get somewhere on a Sunday you spent alone, you passed the green energy guy, who asked then, as always, *are you interested in going green today?*

Without stopping you said, maybe a little abruptly: *Can't stop, sorry.*

In an uncharacteristically assertive moment, he called after you: *Planet can't wait, man.*

You found yourself turning, then starting back on your way.

No. No one is served by getting caught up in this.

But you wheeled around again and walked back past Paul, the bakery, the meat guy. You walked right up to that green energy guy, and sputtered, *you have no idea what anyone does or is up against...man!*

Then you walked away, without listening for a response, and went where you were going.

Boy, did you show him; you are not going green today! You're like, look how not green I am going right now, fucker.

Later you told your son about how you lost your temper and then felt foolish. Now he is worried about what will happen if green energy guy says something to you again and he unconsciously picks up his pace past the stall. Your son is worried you will become The Incredible Hulk. That kind of going green.

You are traipsing together up the block, toward Avenue C, where the water was four feet deep. You will climb the steps, wrestle the keys, lick the crumbs, turn on the music, and turn on the faucet, more awake to the flow of water than you ever thought you'd be.

You get home with bags of food, make lunch. As every week, your son tries to bargain with you for more screen time, eventually gives up and returns to his book about dragons.

You slice a carrot, take a bite, and start handing him pieces, because you know that if you stop to ask, *do you want carrots* he will say no but if you don't ask, he will just eat them. You do not want to be caught in this cliché of small bounties versus nihilistic reality, etc., until you just are.

And anyway what is there left to catch? You are from the Midwest and what is the Midwest except a landscape of small bounties and nihilistic realities? The over-paved prairie and the glassy lake in the morning; the cold politeness, murderous cops, sweaty punk shows; the inside of your body, the years in which your lengthening body cleaved to this landscape and then found solace in this always new city.

The vision of competing pasts, presents and futures pours from your eyes.

You look in your calendar and schedule the arrest. **H**

Zero Hour for the Rabbit

by Jacqueline Ellis

'If you see a rabbit with swollen eyes and sores in between its fur, you should hit it with a brick,' my dad says. 'Put it out of its misery.'

I scan the open mouth of the burrow – it's the size of my nine-year-old foot inside a bright red waterproof boot. There are no black lead-shot-size droppings around, no signs of life.

I rarely saw rabbits on my walks with my parents in Holme Fen woods. I trudged behind them down spongy peat pathways edged with goose grass and stinging nettles. Kept my hands at the sides of my body to avoid the zig-zag leaves that could welt my skin. Muted browns, muddy greens, silver birch tree spindles surrounded me. There were no lush meadows or moss-covered rock groves, no swathes of bluebells or dots of orange-red poppies. No wide-eyed deer or wise owls, no wooden bridges over sparkling streams. Just damp earth and air thick with dandelion spores. Only the sound of my boots flapping against my calves and the repetitive peeps of tiny brown birds among the high leaves.

Our house was built on Coneygree Road – a street name derived from the twelfth-century French word for rabbit warren. Once there had been hundreds, maybe thousands, of rabbits in the spaces that were now roads, gravel front gardens, and cracked concrete street corners. Once, there might have been picture-book meadows outside my bedroom window, filled with plush-furred Disney-cartoon rabbits that scurried back and forth, twitched their ears, stole cabbages, decorated their burrows with miniature furniture made of twigs and acorn shells, had other forest animals over for tea and honey.

On a high school trip to Boulogne, France, I would see dead rabbits hung on hooks in the meat section of a supermarket. They still had their fur. Fluorescent strip lights reflected in their milky-black eyes. Never having seen a rabbit meant to be eaten, I was surprised by their size. Stretched out long from hind legs tied together around hooks to dangling front claws and ear tips. By then, I had eaten river trout, pheasant, even hare, but never rabbit.

In the 1930s, Fenland farmers decided rabbits were pests, not food. Shotguns were inefficient in eradicating them. Instead, gamekeepers used gin traps and laid snares at the edges of burrows and fields. If a snare was too big, rabbits would scuttle busily through. If it was caught, my dad said, a rabbit would sometimes gnaw off its own foot to escape the wire.

In my hometown, rabbits' feet dyed garish colours were sold from market stalls alongside cassette tapes,

Matchbox cars, and cuddly toys made of shiny polyester. You could win them at an amusement arcade in exchange for metal tokens from fruit machines or Roll-a-Ball horse races. Rabbit-foot fobs were attached to school bags or car keychains. Sometimes there'd be little claws among the neon pink or yellow fur, other times the 'foot' was just a cylinder of polystyrene with a piece of fake fur glued around it. The market stall or arcade worker would twirl the rabbit foot around on the key chain, and say, 'A rabbit's foot is good luck.' Then, they would look down at the dismembered paw, or the likeness of one, half-smile and add, 'well, not for the rabbit.'

My dad said that poachers used ferrets to chase rabbits out of their burrows. Caught inside waiting nets, the rabbits would be killed by dogs or shot. Sometimes cyanide gas was fed into the warrens for the rabbits to breathe until they died and could be collected by the dozen. But, as quick as the rabbits could be killed, they bred and multiplied: refilled the landscape, hoovered through crops, ate their way through profits.

The solution was a virus: myxomatosis. In the 1950s, scientists introduced it to England's rabbit population, concentrating their efforts on East Anglia, the peat fenlands where I grew up. Rabbits died by the hundreds, thousands. If our house on Coneygree Road had been built then, I would have seen rabbits dying from the front window: blind, matted fur, slow-motion spiral convulsions. There would have been piles of them – shallow breath, not quite dead – for farmers to clear, to make way for wheat, potatoes, sugar beet, oilseed rape. Myxomatosis was, according to naturalists, zero hour for the rabbit. Ninety-nine percent were exterminated. That was why I had never eaten one. Why I had never seen the tops of their ears in the high grass, never watched their tails bounce away through the trees.

What if, when I turned around from the rabbit hole, I had seen my dad holding a brick? He would have had to bring it specially from work. There were no rocks big enough to crush a rabbit's skull in the woods. What if, when I turned around, he had his arm raised and the brick in his fist? What if his other hand gripped the shuddering rabbit's neck against the ground? What if I watched him slam the brick down onto the rabbit's head and its brains had flecked across his knuckles and onto the cuff-edges of his coat?

I crouch nearer to the hole, place some twigs and pieces of yellow, pulled-up grass at its entrance. I stare into it, squint, afraid to push my fingers into the clammy dark.

I look behind me and my dad is standing straight, looking up toward the sky. His hand is a salute-shade over his eyes. He is deciphering the shape of birds' wings and tails, the placement of their grey feathers, the colour of their beaks. He tells me to hurry up. I am glad that I haven't seen a rabbit that my dad needed to release from its misery. That he had not had to carry out this good deed. That the landscape had stayed barren – austere and flat – relieved of its warmth and joy. **H**

Screw You, Descartes

by Laura Knott

One

My father tries to focus on the plastic braided rug: Blue/white/gray/black. Blue/white/gray/black.

He sits alone, in my step-grandfather's chair, his spine curved, his chin pushed forward, and he looks out toward the floor in front of my grandmother's desk. He commands his hands to rest lightly on his knees. Still, they tremble.

My mother stops me as I run into the room, her fingerpads reaching radius and ulna. I want to reclaim my forearm, but I dare not. There is no need for her to stop me. Once I see him, I can't move.

Organizing her vocal apparatus, my mother squeezes sound past larynx, tongue, teeth, and lips. She says, 'Daddy may not remember much about the last two years.'

My limp father turns his head. He says, 'Hey, Shug.' Shooog. Sugar.

He smiles, small.

I calculate. If he has lost only the past two years, he will remember that Allison has died.

———

Reasons I didn't want to go back to Mississippi:
  1. The man who threatened me with a machete

2. The girl who chased me at recess and, when she caught me, hit hard
3. The teacher who read stories to our third-grade class in 'negro dialect'
4. The man who looked into our windows at night
5. My other classmates, whom, on learning that we would move to North Carolina, I had exhorted to, 'Eat my dust.'

———

My father announces that he is unwell. After breakfast at his colleague's fancy house, somewhere in South Carolina, we turn back, toward Mississippi. My mother drives, my father sleeps in the passenger seat, and my brother and I keep quiet in the back. Instead of returning to the hamlet where we have lived for the past three years, we veer to my father's hometown, further north in north Mississippi.

I breathe.

For three weeks, my brother and I attend school there. I tell the other kids that our father is in the hospital. I don't mention which hospital, or why he is there. As to my lack of information about our mother's whereabouts, I remain silent.

Our uncle tells us jokes that he's heard at the Post Office. Our aunt fries bacon for breakfast. She makes biscuits and she gives us butter and molasses. The bedroom where I sleep is clean. The house is precisely heated. No one chases me.

—

HAM-D scale, developed in 1960:

A score of 20 or higher justifies admission to a mental hospital. Above 23 is 'very severe.' My father's score would have been, perhaps, 31.

BDI-I assessment, introduced in 1961:

Of the four possible responses to the first question, this is the most serious: 'I am so sad and unhappy that I can't stand it.'

Fingers of neurons reach out, searching. For what?

—

Researchers, for hundreds if not thousands of years, have tried to break through depression by inducing convulsions – first with plants and, later, with current. Carrie Fisher, Carrie Mathison, David Foster Wallace, Ernest Hemingway, Esther Greenwood, Kitty Dukakis, Lou Reed, Randle McMurphy, Thomas Eagleton.

My father associated leaving Mississippi with one of his children dying. That's how he explained it to himself, and to me: Why he couldn't keep driving further north that morning. Why he needed to be there, near my sister's bones. And why, by staying near to them, he thought he was protecting me. While I wanted – only – to forget.

Two

Early symptoms of Alzheimer's disease reveal failures of unity in the hippocampus. This area of the human brain – associated with memory and emotion, and affected by electroconvulsive shocks – is also associated with the clear awareness of where and when the person's brain is, in space and time.

—

I parse the instructions for administration and scoring of the Mini-Mental State Examination, the Modified Mini-Mental State Examination, the Mini-Cog^{TM}, and the AD8 Dementia Screening Interview. I believe that I exhibit zero cognitive deficits, though counting backwards by seven is difficult for me. In my defense: it always has been.

I imagine the neurologist calling my mother's name. I imagine my mother's fear, her embarrassment, her effort to hide what she already knew.

Hippocampal. Seahorse-like. Drifting.

On her last trip to the beach, my mother slept through meals and, on waking, ate with ferocious concentration, leaning forward, holding the plate to her chin, scraping food into her mouth. She tried to tell me that she had lost her rings. I found them tucked between her lower lip and gums.

Had she known her circumstances in those last years, the humiliation alone would have killed her.

When she began to fall sideways out of her recliner, my father couldn't keep her at home any longer.

The thermostat in the nursing home was set high. The windows were closed and locked. We punched a four-digit code to open the unit door. None of the patients could remember it. Or the smell of fresh air.

anticonvulsants	bandages	bedrails
bedsores	cleaning solutions	disposable diapers
exhalations	IV bags	nitrile gloves
overcooked peas	plastic furniture	plastic tubing
rubber sheets	sour washcloths	stainless steel needles
vitamin pills	whimpers	despair

The last time I saw my mother alive, her nervous system was misfiring. She was lying in a hospital bed, where she had been for six months, and shuddering every few seconds, as if she were suddenly cold, then suddenly cold, then suddenly cold. As if there were nothing else. As if there never had been.

My mother was napping. She had not spoken for days. When she woke, she turned her head toward mine, and she said, 'You cryin'?'

Three

Alzheimer's ✔	anxiety ✔	depression ✔
hearing loss ✔	migraine ✔	sleep disorders ✔
stroke ✔	tinnitus ✔	vision loss ✔

Four

A depressive man burrows into his habits of
thought. He races in place, fearful, instilling fear.
A woman with Alzheimer's disease disconnects.
She is unable to form thoughts. She, too, is fearful,
instilling fear. Leaks seep under the walls and
spring through the cracks: loss, shame, care,
suffering, pain.

When the neuroscientists investigate memory,
they ask, 'Did the engineered rodent turn, correctly,
to the right or, incorrectly, to the left?' And when
they test depression, they ask, 'Did the engineered
rodent give up and sink, or did she keep swimming?'

They don't ask what panic the rodent might feel.
What valor? What determination to connect? Or,
when thinking breaks, what continues, un-thought? **H**

My Stepfather, Bolton's Entire First Eleven at the '95 Play-Off Final Against Reading

by Jordan Harrison-Twist

1. Keith Branagan
First, we must learn spelling rules, like the one
about the double consonants after short vowels,
and the *i-before-e* business with the weird exception.
Keith – that was one of them, too – would come to
teach at that school my stepfather cared so much
about. You know. *That* kind of school.

2. Scott Green
The way he leant his full weight against the
upholstery after eating, belly rolled like truckers'
arms through the slats. And when it buckles and he
falls through French doors onto glass, my mother's
anther hands pull above him the way Green kicked
at vacant air after he'd lost his man, knowing that
there would be consequences. But there was no time
to warn him. No time to escape the laughter or the
reach of his palm. It had already happened.

3. Jimmy Phillips
Up and out – and I know the comparison of the man
who does the ugly things well, a world of pressure
through a stud onto a doughy and talented toe,
and I'm thirteen, and I'm working, because – *I'll
not be paying for that school if you don't pull your weight.*
It is something about him I grudgingly respect:
he is, unlike my blood dad, a man eddied into life
in the black morning's vapours. And the same
Sunday I pick toilet rolls and soaps from warehouse
shelves, he has found time for church. Hoping his
Christianity will save him from me, his gruff tenor
pulling harmonies from closely guarded secrets, and
he is now, in front of me at the warehouse, for the
first time in our year's acquaintance, about to go
off (something wild) at Carol and Shaz in high-vis
smocks smoking the last of their L&Bs at the shutter,
and at me for letting them, the fucking dossers,
the lot of you. And I say something hurtful about
swearing and heaven and what Jesus would want.

4. Jason McAteer
Incisive and *pass*, he says, or rather we say,
sequentially, as he thumbs out the skeleton from
the salmon's flesh and grows scales on his palm
heel, *incisive, don't you think*; and I say *pass*, because
fish still smells like fish and still looks like fish, and

I've only just begun to eat food that touches on the plate, never mind this thing that – even before it has died – favours a corpse, or an error of his god's judgment.

5. Gudni Bergsson

The older I get, the more gifts come to look like books, and if he happens upon an anthology (which as good as selects itself every year), so much the better. As reliable as the old Fin with clearances, it will be the cartoonist's Best Of for birthdays. And he signs it *love Dad*. Which I don't acknowledge.

6. Alan Stubbs

I imagine that I, instead, had wheeled my piano into the family, crushing old roots to culture fingers. Every day, to wake and dispense new customs with the oranges and the oats, the apples with the bruises cut out, met with the glare of a boy, a strapping lad, the centre of a back three, who kicks away with baby feet, baby feet I was not there to talc. Or see grow into barricades.

7. Neil McDonald

He went off halfway through. The substitute, as all substitutes, a calculated risk. An expectation that it will take to the play, the way hewn limbs feel their way back into foreign bodies. The replacement is a cultured fellow and has a good mind, is in all the right places – and the way he does all of that running so that I don't have to, and protects my body from the accusations and the screech of floodlights. And smiles sweetly at my *He's not—* to their *Your dad's pretty old isn't he.*

8. Owen Coyle
When the sled broke the ice on the lodge, and the last I saw was those pink fingers and my brother's mouth so wide and futile, as the staid lungs tensed out all their breath, and a man who could not swim cutting out like the blade of a knife, holding the little body a foot above his submerged head, in celebration, some ribboned and spluttering cup, and I think no man should risk so much to be noticed by his son.

9. Mixu Paatelainen
A man strong as the heart of the matter, and softly proximal, a distant kind of always there. He throws himself at every loose ball with the ferocity of memories replicating themselves. So we behave as he did with our hatred of large-knotted ties, of slovenly dropped consonants, and our need to be seen clearly by those who love us. To be seen as strong as the heart of the matter. Even if that heart is homesick for other sons. So we hold him upright, and learn to call him father.

10. John McGinlay
The body has rebuked him and it has him scratching at all hours and the insides of his mouth have come away, leaving him a ravaged man, who chooses words with care to their painful aspirates,

and chooses not to eat at all. But I say Super John wore gloves once when the keeper was sent packing for a bad foul, and he donned them and did well, conceding nothing, saving all he could. And he nods and puts on mittens as if I were his mother. Conceding nothing.

11. Alan Thompson

There is not one heretic amongst the group of eleven that played and won in '95. All portions of the same entity, same whim, same Thommo, who sent that force on its way. And not one in eleven, when there are cheers to be had, for whom there would be a better conversation than a familiar conversation, and no more familiar conversation than one about football. And no conversation about football not worth having. ⊞

Robinson
Daniel

Jennifer Crusoe

by Jenn Ashworth

Dear Prudence,

We don't know each other yet, so I'll start by saying that a few years ago I made a New Year's resolution to send thank you letters to the authors of books that I'd read. One of the early letters I wrote was to Yiyun Li, who wrote *Dear Friend, from My Life I Write to You in Your Life;* a memoir of a two-year period in which she suffered severe depression.

The memoir is an exploration of the give-and-take of reading and Li describes the book as one half of a conversation with her editor, Brigid Hughes. The title is taken from a phrase unearthed from Katherine Mansfield's journals and a journal is, as Bram Stoker's Mina Harker said, just one way of speaking and listening at the same time.

In my letter, I wrote about the parts of Li's book that I'd underlined and found myself reading repeatedly, trying to learn them by heart, wanting to get the words she'd written to become part of my body. Her depiction of depression as a kind of autoimmune disease where the mind turns on itself was particularly affecting. Li wrote back, pleased with my thank you note, and mentioned something about the years-long conversation with a book that re-reading can be. That small encouragement started a habit that helped me think more clearly about the exchange of reading. Maybe, I found myself hoping, writing thank you letters might help fix what years of grading student work had done to my mind – turning every occasion of reading into a fault-finding mission. What would happen if I turned up to every book requiring myself to be pleased, and searching for what pleased me?

My point is, Prudence, there's an underlying selfishness to my gratitude. There is also a greediness to it: I turn up to my books these days wanting to take something from them for myself; there's not only a willingness to be fed but an expectation of it.

Jennifer

Dear Prudence,

Earlier this year, my mother came to visit me and
brought with her a box she'd found in her attic. It
wasn't a box I'd forgotten about: for twenty years
I've held the memory of my eighteen-year-old self
packing up some things in the flat I was living in
before leaving Preston to move to Cambridge for
university.

The adults around me were suddenly and
unusually impressed and offered confusing pieces
of advice. I was going off to 'become someone'
and, to achieve this, I should try to fit in. Nobody
I knew had been to Cambridge, but they seemed
to know how I should disguise myself: I should
moderate my Northern accent, ditch the Marilyn
Manson T-shirt, stop smoking and swearing and
be a bit more grateful. On top of that, I should also
never forget where I came from. This would involve
preserving myself, as if in amber. I might be going
off to become someone, but I was also 'nobody
special', had no business forgetting it and should
be really careful not to come back talking like a
toff. There was a violence to these instructions –
however well-meant or jokingly delivered – that I
felt but did not understand.

The girl who packed the box knew this move
across the country was a big deal. There was no
going back; I had no childhood bedroom to scuttle
back to when term was over. The things inside the
box were like the vowels I should both ditch and
keep. It was all stuff that would both give me away

and keep me tethered – ballast and anchor. I saw
that girl pack it up and mail it to her future self in
a journey that would take twenty years. And here it
was, returned to me, sealed tightly in brown tape,
then wrapped in a couple of bin bags. The brown
tape and the black bags gave the thing a certain look:
a corpse dismembered and prepared for dumping
on a motorway verge somewhere out of town.

> **I saw that girl pack it up and mail it
> to her future self in a journey
> that would take twenty years**

Here's Yiyun Li, reflecting in English from
her life in America on her own relation to China,
her family of origin and her mother tongue. She's
an example of the American dream – leaving a
traumatic past Somewhere Else behind in order
to assimilate into the English language, western
literary culture, a kind of 'nothingness' of a life
disguised in fiction: 'One marks oneself a rebel
and a castaway simultaneously when renouncing a
belief,' (p.95) she writes. And when the box arrived,
it was as if my little rebel-castaway had sent me a
message in a bottle.

Jennifer

Dear Prudence

I wrote about your novel once, you know. In my own memoir-in-essays, *Notes Made While Falling*, I describe it badly, forgetting many of the characters and condensing your storyline with my own. I describe your protagonist (whose name I could not remember, nor the title of the book) as 'a shadow or a kind of foggy darkness seeping out from under the crack in his bedroom door.' (p.67)

This discussion takes place in the context of my reflecting on a question I was often asked once I washed up at university to study English Literature. 'And did you have many books, growing up, at home?' people would ask – sometimes mere seconds after I opened my mouth (p.66). And I knew precisely and exactly what they meant and had no idea how to answer what they were actually asking, other than to fantasise about describing a novel I did have as a child – your novel – but had since lost and could hardly remember. I don't even give your name in my book, because I didn't know it.

A handful of times over the last couple of years someone who has read that passage has sent me a Facebook message with a picture of a novel or a link to an Amazon page and asked,

'Is this the one?'

I'd click through or examine the picture as if I'd been presented with evidence of a lost loved one. I desperately wanted to have the opportunity for gratitude and, each time, resented being disappointed.

'No, that's not it,' I'd say.

I started to wonder if I was making things up. The man I live with has a joke that is too long-winded to explain here but the punchline rests on my inability to distinguish between what I imagine and what I remember.

> **'Are we talking *inside-real* or *outside-real*,' he says, when I start telling him what happened at work...**

'Are we talking *inside-real* or *outside-real*,' he says, when I start telling him what happened at work, or about some chapter I'm about to write.

The thing is, I don't always know. The border between inside and outside is a little leaky where I'm concerned. The edges of all territories require some violence, or at the very least an effort I am unwilling to expend, in order to maintain them. The book I treasured though I could not remember – well – it could have been inside-real only. I did start to think that.

Jennifer

Dear Prudence,

You'll have seen this coming, but indulge me. Would you believe me if I told you when I opened the box and saw your novel sitting there inside, tucked between (I'm sorry about this) Marilyn Manson's ghost-written autobiography *The Long Hard Road Out of Hell* (I know, I know) and a copy of *The Omen* (I shit you not) that the hairs on the back of my neck stuck up (a cliché – I am sorry about that too) and the whole thing felt like an out-of-body experience?

Robinson Daniel Crusoe, a strange book about a clever boy called Daniel Talbot, told by his younger brother Jimmy. Daniel is the son of a neurotic, largely absent mother (she walks the dog a lot) and a man desperate to transcend his working-class origins. Daniel Talbot is supposed to go to a good grammar, then Oxbridge, then to 'become someone'. And as soon as he gets wind of the plan his father has for him, he refuses school, camps out in a garden shed, fakes illness, writes a diary in which he pretends to be Robinson Crusoe and eventually finds his own escape by building a raft and setting sail – not to discover new lands or inhabit tropical islands, but to drown in the Mersey. The brother narrates the period after his death with thinly disguised relief. Daniel was so clever, and so mad, and such a massive, massive pain in the arse. Such a bloody ungrateful son.

Jennifer

Dear Prudence,

It is indecorous to share what else was inside that box, but as it is just between us, I will.

First, a letter, written in an old fashioned and trembling hand, from a woman married to a man my mum was sort-of-seeing. This woman was sick, expecting to die (as far as I know she's still alive) and, in a piece of advance planning from beyond-the-grave (this side, not the other side), lining up my mother as her husband's next wife.

None of us, Mormons though we were, were so innocent that we didn't know what a blow job was

This woman had received reports from her husband that I had been resisting his attempts to be friendly. The gift of two Wishbone Ash albums, recorded from CD onto tape so I could listen to them on my personal stereo, had been cruelly rejected. The offer of an occasional lift somewhere or other in his Fiesta had been declined with derision. This guy's second name began with a 'J' and because the traditions of the religion we were all in at that time meant we addressed him as 'Brother' I'd decided to call him 'BJ'. To his face. None of us, Mormons though we were, were so innocent that we didn't know what a blow job was.

'All right, BeeJay?' I'd cry cheerily, at the sight of him sitting in his car, waiting outside the train station for me. He'd flinch, and grin, and open his glove compartment to show me some new CDs he'd set aside.

'He won't hurt you,' his wife had written, urging me to stop being a spanner in the works and give BeeJay a chance. I'd have been fourteen at the time. I was extremely inconvenient. 'He won't lift a hand to you,' she'd said. 'He's never hit me; he's never struck our children.'

Jennifer

Dear Prudence,

Once a letter is addressed to you, and sent to you, it's up to you what you do with it, isn't it? I don't mean legally. I mean morally. Because there were a few letters in that box from my father, who did not write very well, asking in an increasingly aggressive and manipulative and – frankly – creepy manner, why I did not want to see him. It was shocking to see these. I'd convinced myself that the casting-away was mutual – that I had been as unwanted a daughter as I was a rejecting one. But no, there he is, promising me presents and asking me if I used hand cream because boys liked it when girls had nice soft hands. 'Why won't you come and visit your old dad?' he asks. The answer to his letter would have been the letter itself. *This is why*, I'd have said. *You're why. Read yourself!*

Jennifer

Dear Prudence,

Anyway. The other paperwork in the box – a few letters and minutes of meetings concerning me but not addressed to me – were from meetings and child protection conferences held by social services and presented a strange opportunity to follow my own advice and *read myself.*

There was a letter from a psychologist I was sent to be cured of school-refusal and violent rages that said I was too disturbed to be helped.

There were minutes of meetings held at a children's home I had been living at for a while that show I'd been invited into the room where the meeting was being held, then asked to wait outside, to 'protect her from the difficult feelings of the adults.'

A lone social worker wondered in writing if my behaviour was actually symptomatic of a marital problem.

A couple of doctors wondered about medication they might try or should not have tried on me and speculated about phobias I may or may not have had.

I was 'disturbed'. The word cropped up a couple of times. I gather from this that they, all these adults around me, had been disturbed by me.

Are these my documents or are they just about me? Why did I have them and why had I kept them and what was I supposed to do with them?

Jennifer

Dear Prudence,

I took photographs of some of the things that were inside the box and sent them to a few friends. 'This is outside-real,' I told myself. 'It definitely, really is.' That was one of the things my younger self was telling me: *these things really happened. Here are the things that made you.*

Once I'd received the message, I set about disposing of the evidence. I put your novel on my bedside table and gave the other, lesser paperbacks to the British Heart Foundation, which is the nearest charity shop to my house. There were a few VHS tapes too – stuff recorded from the telly before the idea of Netflix was a twinkle in anyone's eye. No charity shop wants them, and you can't even recycle them: guiltily, I put the legacy, obsolete media in the bin. Then I burned every single bit of paper left in the box. I crouched at the hearth like Cinderella in my big kitchen in front of the big middle-class log burner I do not know how to be grateful for, watching the flames eat it up and wondering if I'd regret it in the morning.

I didn't. Once a message has been received there's no need to linger at the scene of the crime waiting to be caught, is there? The book – your book – I carried around with me for days. I read, re-read, remembered. Was remembered. A book, I discovered (I already knew), can see the parts of you that you've chopped off, wrapped in plastic and prepared for disposal.

Jennifer

Dear Prudence,

I don't think I'm getting anywhere near what I want to say. I'm not even circling it. There's a note in the front of your novel from the publisher that I'd never noticed as kid. Why would I have? Heinemann speaks on your behalf and says: 'the author would like to draw the reader's attention to the passages from *Robinson Daniel Crusoe's Diary* which are not direct quotations from *Robinson Crusoe*' and now I come to think of that, the weirdness of it that little denial-before-the-fact, it comes to remind me of the tricksy note Defoe prefaces his Crusoe with. He says, 'the Editor believes the thing to be a History of Fact; neither is there any Appearance of Fiction in it: And whoever thinks, because all such things are dispatch'd, that the Improvement of it, as well as to the Diversion as to the Instruction of The Reader, will be the same.'

Why did you bother? He was out of copyright – nobody was going to sue

Defoe wasn't much bothered about the difference between outside-real or inside-real either, and you – or your publisher – wanted to draw attention to the fact that though it might seem you'd lifted some of the passages of Daniel's strange journal directly from Defoe, you hadn't. Why did you bother? He was out of copyright – nobody was going to sue.

I've been thinking for ages about the difficult ways these things slot together: the way Defoe has his Crusoe educate Friday, and also live dependent on Friday's knowledge and expertise. The white supremacy of it. That education as a concept is a civilisation project – one which the civilisee must be grateful for, even if both the process of education and the state of being grateful for it feels like chopping off the unacceptable parts of yourself and forgetting about them/treasuring them/putting them in a box.

You understood that – and showed Daniel's violent refusal of it in ways that were bound to make us take his side. He's tragic and selfish and funny – forging notes, faking pneumonia and even blindness to get out of school – and his father is crazy and manipulative and controlling, mocking Daniel's refusal in rants about 'gratitude and children of today.' (p.36)

But as Daniel defies his father and privately imagines himself as rebel and castaway in diary entries written through Defoe ('In good faith, Robinson Daniel Crusoe could do with a miracle now,' (p.135) he writes, on the day his father sends him to a psychiatrist) you also decide to complicate matters. During the day while he's skipping school, Daniel takes up with a kid who lives in a council flat, whose father and brothers don't have jobs, who nicks things and rides his bike around when he's supposed to be at school, and who can't read.

In the scenes where Daniel is with this kid – Barry – he's at his most unsympathetic and unpleasant – patronising, snobbish, cold. 'But you must work at your reading Barry, if you want to become fluent,' (p.87) this Crusoe says to his Man Friday. Barry can get Daniel things that he needs – things to build a raft – and so Daniel takes up smoking and carries on the reading lessons. 'I have to join in what Barry does or I can't help him. But I don't really mean it. It's different for me,' (p.87) Daniel says, when his younger brother asks him what he's playing at. He speaks as if he's Defoe and emphasises gratitude and debt: 'He really is a most dextrous fellow. He has a strong obligation to me,' and at times compares his do-gooding to another of his heroes – St Francis of Assisi. That's right – the saint who was kind to animals. It's creepy and unpleasant, watching Daniel becoming just like his father. As a reader, I don't know where to put myself. Where I'm supposed to be lodging my love. And this is before we know what Daniel's plan is and what he wants this raft for.

In her book *Appropriate: A Provocation*, Paisley Rekdal starts by acknowledging the complex problem of what happens when we write through or about what we don't or can't know, and what ethical and cultural complexities take place in the formal hinterlands of works which draw on or adapt others. When Defoe wrote Friday, or when you lifted and repurposed Defoe's novel for your own purposes, both of you are engaging in a technically and ethically complex act of cultural exchange. Sometimes there's not much 'give' and the act is a brutal kind of taking – a theft that causes harm – and at other times, the work is a more intellectually engaged 'cultural approximation' (p.13) which Rekdal describes as a giving and taking where the writer is both agent and subject. It's the opposite of autoimmunity, this – Yiyun Li's model of depression as a condition where the mind, sealed and turned inwards, starts to feed on itself. This is transfusion.

Redkal explains it better: 'There's a porousness that occurs between reader and writer. The writer shapes a character the reader is invited to see herself in relation to, and in doing so, the reader gives herself up to the text; she relaxes some aspect of her own identity when reading a character. [...] As a reader, I allow my imagination to become a thing grafted upon by another mind.' (p.152-3)

And this is where the great difficulty of gratitude comes in: nobody is unimaginable, and nobody is without the need to see themselves imagined

But Prudence, I am left with some questions.

Can we love something without appropriating it?

How do we love something and keep a proper respectful distance?

Can we graft and be grafted upon – an invasive, foolish intimacy – and not hurt each other?

Would you think with me for a little while, about the relation of the original to the copy to the remix to the cover version?

About adaptations and shipwrecks?

About what it is for one life to be confiscated by another – what kind of sin appropriation is, and what kind of love?

And this is where the great difficulty of gratitude comes in: nobody is unimaginable, and nobody is without the need to see themselves imagined.

Jennifer

Dear Prudence,

Do you know, I don't even know what you look like? What kind of colleague or fan or stalker am I? It's a poor showing. I want to put a face to your name and have you in my mind's eye. I googled you first thing, of course. There was a tiny black-and-white thumbnail image of a face with dark hair.

I tried Amazon for it, and the only listing was for a second-hand copy from the US, but you were listed as Pyramid Andrews

Underneath was your name, which I already knew, and 'Born 1924: aged 97 years.' I clicked through to see the photograph more clearly but the image turned out to be the cover of one of your books and the face on that cover belonged to a boy in his teens, staring out angrily past the camera. The book was called *Goodbye to the Rat* and the synopsis said it was a novel about a group of young working-class men leaving school and struggling to find work in the late 1970s. I tried Amazon for it, and the only listing was for a second-hand copy from the US, but you were listed as Pyramid Andrews.

Jennifer

Dear Pyramid Scheme,

You put Daniel's name right there, inside Robinson
Crusoe's, right on the front cover of the book. Daniel
both is and is not Crusoe, and writes through him,
impersonates Defoe's style in his own diary, and
also is written by you to be like him – that strange,
sometimes coercive, often co-dependent friendship
with a young man from the wrong side of town.
Daniel's younger brother has his nose put out, because
Daniel, every inch the white saviour, has got himself
a new Friday – someone to educate into gratitude.
Daniel imagines himself as a saint, sometimes:
but isn't this sickly expectation of gratitude what
happens when you try very hard to be good when
really you don't want to be? The world has to owe
you something for the sacrifice you've made.

Isn't it weird that I, who refused school until the
very last minute then turned up, resentfully, to take
the GCSE exams just to prove that I could, and get
out of there to somewhere else, ended up as a teacher?
I teach Creative Writing, which apparently is a racket
aimed at keeping writers who can't make any money
from their own work off the streets. We dish out
degrees like sweeties, awarding many more than there
ever will be jobs. It's a Ponzi scheme, exploitative,
just plain wrong. I think all the time about where I
lead my students, or what it is I can give them, and
how to be grateful for the opportunity.

Cynthia Cruz in her book *The Melancholia of Class*
writes about what happens when working-class
people make their unwelcome and ungrateful entries

into the middle-class world. She's especially good on the special weirdness that happens when someone like me stands at the front of a class. 'When I am teaching, I am neither who I am (working class), nor who I am attempting to pass as (middle class). How do I teach, then, as a ghost? How do I exist?' (p.102)

I think you must have been a teacher too, alongside your writing. Something about the way you write young people, disturbed or disturbing or at the very least ungrateful, and the attention you pay to the professionals around them – the social workers, doctors, careers advisors and teachers – makes me think you were in the know. I had an educational welfare officer. A social worker. I had all sorts. I was in the know too.

Jennifer

Dear Prudence,

Once, I was in a room being interviewed by an educational psychologist I'd been sent to see. Do you remember the part of your book where Daniel is sent to see someone about his school refusing? They try all sorts of stuff with him – making him draw pictures, or speak about his dreams, or give him hard consequences and sending his psychiatrist to haul him to school in a taxi. Prudence, you are so funny about the medicalisation of distress and refusal – I know you'd have been on my side. Daniel has been teasing these doctors by gratifying them with entirely made-up dreams with sexual undertones, but late on in the book they're onto him, and threaten to inject him with a drug that will force him to tell them the truth.

... I asked – not quite innocently – if I'd be given injections to make me tell the truth

When I was presented as a problem to the NHS, I asked – not quite innocently – if I'd be given injections to make me tell the truth. I wanted them to know I was onto them: I knew their methods. My psychologist laughed and asked me where I'd got the idea about injections from. I clammed up. What would I have said? That *you* were where I'd got the idea from? That I'd read this novel about a boy who was like me and not like me? I didn't have the words for what was wrong with me but for the first time in my life I could have, in answer to a question about who or what I was, pointed at a book. Your book.

Then this psychologist did something even more astonishing. She asked me what I wanted to lie about. She was sharp, that one. I was not used to adults getting the better of me and the fact that she had before I'd even had chance to get my coat off made me like her.

'*Everything,*' I said. 'I want to lie about everything.'

She only smiled at that. I refused to speak to her, and she discharged me as her patient after a couple more fruitless appointments. I don't regret it, but I can think now of things that I could have said. I could have read to her.

You won't get this now, I could have said – to her and to me – *but books will wait for as long as you need them to.*

Jennifer

Dear Prudence,

You're a hard woman to find. My internet digging says you have connections to Liverpool, and this novel does too. Are you a Northerner like me? If I knocked on your door and asked you to sign the book that I both lost, forgot about and treasured, would you answer? Do you have a Liverpool accent? Did anyone ever tell you to lose it/keep it?

There's a bit in your novel where we find out Daniel's dad isn't someone big in accounts at his workplace, he's just been telling everyone that, and instead he works in the warehouse and wears an overall. 'I didn't go to night school, and I don't have any diplomas. I haven't got an office job. I don't even count as white collar.' (p.71)

He's spent his whole life faking, and all that fakery did was make him both invisible to his family, and an intrusive burden they're all relieved to be rid of when he finally does the decent thing and dies, towards the end of the novel – too late for Daniel, of course.

Being grateful is a difficult thing for a working-class person. You're supposed to climb that social mobility ladder under your own steam, just to prove to the lazy peasants who languish at the bottom of it that it can be done. When you get to the top, as compliantly transformed as Cinderella, who is there to be grateful to? Better to be as ghostly as Cynthia Cruz suggests, so as not to cause any damage to anyone. 'What happens to the working-class subject while they're masked in the persona of another, more palatable self?' (p.122) she asks. Eventually, she argues there's a cracking, a splitting – and breakup/breakdown happens.

For a while I wanted to know how you knew about what it felt like to pretend to wear the suit you're not allowed to want and be stuck in the overall anyway. If you had diplomas and a white-collar job. If when you were a teacher, you had ever forced someone else to be grateful for what you forced down their throat instead of taking for yourself.

I think of Daniel's father – his respectability, his rages and nosebleeds and his heart attacks. Daniel (and me) ricocheting between rebellion and submission and his eventual suicide. No matter how responsible you try to be about that storyline, Prudence, knowing this is a book written for children, it's hard for me to read Daniel's 'misadventure' as anything other than a glorious magic exit – the nothing-flavoured sweet spot between resisting and giving in. I think of what breaking down, splitting up, being wounded and gratitude have in common with each other: both ways of piercing, wounding, bringing the outside in.

Jennifer

Dear Prudence,

I'd call you Ms Andrews, I think, if I wrote to you.
Otherwise you might think I was making fun of you
by invoking the song. Maybe I'd email you. Or your
agent. *Hi*, I'd type. *Hello Ms Andrews. Prudence, if I
may?* But now *Dear Prudence* is in my head, singing
you up into being like the morning.

For a while, I imagine you as a teenager, buying
The White Album and lifting the needle to hear the song
with your name. Maybe your friends sang it at you.
Were they kind and did it make you laugh, and feel
special and chosen and famous? Did it feel cruel to
you? Apparently, George and John wrote this song to
coax Prudence Farrow out of her cottage, where she
had lost her mind after a long time sitting meditating
in the dark during a summer of Transcendental
Meditation training with the Maharishi at Rishikesh.
Everyone was worried about her. Did you have
a darkened-room moment of your own – an
autoimmune problem caused by a sealed shut self?
Did you put something of yourself into Daniel,
who built a raft and pretended he was escaping the
confines of his life but was only killing himself?

Did you have a darkened-room moment of your own – an autoimmune problem caused by a sealed shut self?

You were forty-four when *The White Album* came
out. Just a tiny bit older than I am now. Perhaps
it passed you by entirely, because you'd have been
busy writing – maybe late at night when your

children were asleep, not using the typewriter in case it woke them, scratching away on a piece of paper in a darkened room.

Even though the song was written for her and played outside the cottage she was staying in, embracing the existential nothing, transcendentally meditating herself into and out of existence, Prudence Farrow didn't remember the song at all. I imagine her like I imagined Daniel; a dark foggy presence, more of a cloud than a person, seeping through a crack in the door. It was a surprise to her, she said, to hear her name being sung on the radio by a few guys she considered friends of hers when it was released later that year.

Jennifer

Dear Prudence, *(won't you come out to play?)*

Listen. Don't worry. I'm not asking to be invited in.
We've both read *Misery*, I presume. I know the types
of hospitality some readers ask for, and the limits to
what a writer can offer. We are inside each other,
you and I, but it doesn't mean that I get to knock
on your front door and expect to be invited in for
tea and a tour of your office and a flick through the
printed-out pages of your work in progress and to
sit on the candlewick bedspread on your bed and
to hold your hand and ask you about your islands,
your rafts, your secret hurts and darkened rooms. I
only want you to tell me about myself anyway. I'm
sure you thought of all this when considering Defoe,
though him being dead must have helped a bit.

Jennifer

Dear Prudence,

I'd like to send you a picture of me so you know what I look like so you can see me in your mind's eye and carry my face in your heart. If we ever meet, at least you'll know who to look out for. But what to send? For a memoirist I have a more ambivalent relationship with the 'selfie' than is decent. The truth is, I'm less keen on my face than I used to be.

For a memoirist I have a more ambivalent relationship with the 'selfie' than is decent

Things are falling down a bit now. People used to say, 'gosh, you don't seem old enough to have done such and such a thing,' and I'd make a joke about a picture in the attic, which sometimes they'd get and sometimes they wouldn't. And all that time it was *you* up there in the attic; or my mother's attic, at least. People aren't saying that so much these days and in the next year or two I may have a midlife crisis, though I'm not sure what form that takes for a woman novelist: the genre seems to belong to men. I digress. My face. It's fallen in and down a bit now, but when you look at the picture enclosed (attached?) try to see me as I was when we first met. Remember me as I was then, because when I was fourteen, I had the best scowl in Preston, the cheek to call an Elder of the one true church 'BeeJay' *to his face* and eyes you could sharpen knives with. Did you know me back then? I think if you'd have known me you'd have liked me, is what I'm saying. I think if you were a teacher and I'd have been in your class, you'd have given me a note for PE and written me as a disturbed character in one of your books, even though it would have been one of the bad kinds of appropriation. I'd have been annoying and stubborn and far, far too big for my boots but if I'd have come across myself later in life and recognised my own face hidden between your lines, I'd have forgiven the trespass as I know I'd be able to tell by the song of the sentences that I'd been loved.

Jennifer

Dear Prudence,

I can't find my point, but I am tired now and I will have to stop soon and will post this anyway and hope it reaches you in your life, where you are, from where I am, in mine, as Katherine Mansfield and Yiyun Li said and have helped me to say.

I have tried hard to be grateful, and I am. I have noted carefully what I have received from you and how useful it has been for me. But the best gratitude is selfish, you see – though I am not entirely myself and neither are you.

I also know that nothing has changed hands, and that nothing you gave me was yours in the first place. The practice of this gratitude – and some days, like today, I feel it swelling up in my head like an empty bubble – reminds me that what I am (my ingredients, and the forces that formed them) is beyond the influence of my own endeavours and always was.

What are you? You're a mind-reader, a clairvoyant, a fortune-teller, a witch. You have written me

And you: I am hoping this letter finds you well. How are you? What are you? You're a mind-reader, a clairvoyant, a fortune-teller, a witch. You have written me. Or you're a nothing: only a channel for Defoe and the world to have their way with me, who turns out to be a no-one, not a someone; nothing much to write home about.

'What a long way it is from one life to another,' wrote Yiyun Li. A distance that requires a letter, and no distance at all, of course.

I'm going to try not to read too much into this. Thank you.

Jennifer

Bibliography

Ashworth, Jenn. *Notes Made While Falling*. Goldsmiths (2019)
Andrew, Prudence. *Robinson Daniel Crusoe*. Heinemann (1978)
Cruz, Cynthia. *The Melancholia of Class: A Manifesto For the Working Class*. Repeater (2021)
Defoe, Daniel. *Robinson Crusoe*, ed. Michael Shinagel. Norton (1994)
Li, Yiyun. *Dear Friend, from My Life I Write to You in Your Life*. Hamish Hamilton (2017)
Redkal, Paisely. *Appropriate: A Provocation*. Norton (2021)

Short online creative writing courses

Make 2022 your writing year — book now for January!

- Study online at any time from the comfort of home
- Fully tutored, receive individual feedback on your work
- Small, friendly groups – 15 students max
- Courses include creative non-fiction and memoir
- Beginner and intermediate levels available
- Co-designed with the University of East Anglia

Beginning January 2022 – book soon!

nationalcentreforwriting.org.uk/creative-writing-online/

'The materials were excellent and the tutor feedback was so helpful. I feel I have learned such a lot and my writing has definitely improved as a result.'

Lisa Tippings, Start Writing Creative Non-Fiction student

Something

Happened

by Alice Kent

If you were wondering, the best time of the week to send out a sales E-newsletter is 11am on a Tuesday. This time generates maximum *Return on Investment (ROI)*. Whenever I say ROI in a meeting, I can't resist a little lip curl. I could have ROI engraved on my tombstone. Ludwig Boltzmann, the grandfather of quantum theory, had $S = k \ log \ W$ engraved on his tombstone; his formula for entropy. It led Einstein to reveal time to be an illusion. There is no such thing as now. So, in effect, it doesn't matter when you send out the sales E-newsletter.

I thought perhaps I'd try to understand quantum theory, and had imagined it may take a few evenings. I'd start with the formula for entropy. How hard could it be? It's only got three letters in it and a log. And I know what a log is. But I quickly found out that there are whole worlds hiding in those letters. For instance, k is defined as:

$$k = 1.380649 \times 10^{-23} \, \text{J.K}^{-1}$$

After four minutes, I gave up trying to understand quantum theory, and wondered about getting into making fresh pasta instead.

I learnt about Tuesdays being the best day to send out a sales E-newsletter at the 'Level One Marketing' evening course I went on several years ago. I've never quite been able to remember though if it's the best time of the week to send out a sales E-newsletter, or if I had imagined this top tip, and it's actually the most common time of the week for suicide. In a fifteen-year career in marketing it's never seemed relevant. But then nothing has seemed very relevant. Relevant to what, I suppose.

Boltzmann killed himself on a Wednesday.

—

The universe is made of stories, not of atoms.

writes Muriel Rukeyser in her poem *The Speed of Darkness.*

The current mania for stories irritates me; companies recruiting for 'Storytellers' to cloak money-stuffing greed behind their heart-warming brand story of Grandma Eileen and her ol' pepper sauce.

With low expectations, I searched for the rest of the poem. These are the first lines:

Whoever despises the clitoris despises the penis
Whoever despises the penis despises the cunt
Whoever despises the cunt despises the life of the child.

Resurrection music,   silence,   and surf.

In 1905, a 26-year-old Einstein had an idea. A beautifully simple idea. He saw that there is no such thing as a universal now. Time does not exist in space. Space and time are one thing. Spacetime, the fabric of reality, bends and is slowed down by objects such as suns and planets. Einstein saw this, aged 26, through vision, and then worked out the maths to prove it. It's said that Einstein didn't like Beethoven and took inspiration from Mozart, whose music he thought 'so pure it seemed to have been ever-present in the universe, waiting to be discovered by its master.'

The music stirs emotions that cannot be named in words; the emotions exist only in and through the music

When watching a film of Daniel Barenboim play the *Appassionata*, I feel an absence of not being with something I love. Whether this is for Barenboim himself, or Beethoven, or for something else, I'm not sure. Perhaps it is for not being able to grasp, define or feel anything with a weight that feels appropriate.

It has been said that Beethoven's music 'exposes the dynamics of emotion without our being able to name the emotions other than the ways the music makes them emerge'. This stuns me. The music stirs emotions that cannot be named in words; the emotions exist only in and through the music. It seems to me; this is the reason for the feeling of absence.

There is a moment in the recording – during the final movement, *allegro ma non troppo*, fast, but not so much so – when Barenboim looks up from the piano to the ceiling of the Vienna concert hall, and seems to plead for something. In that moment he translates something I can feel with a weight that seems appropriate.

It was through not thinking that Einstein saw the way the universe works. In turning off the brain's need to translate thinking into words, he created the space to see reality. This gets close perhaps to what it is to be a less-conscious animal; to live without thinking. To know, as the robin knows how to navigate its migration through the magnetic field of the Earth.

Ludwig Boltzmann – the short, awkward Austrian, grandfather of quantum theory – devoted his life, *his life*, to the single question: 'Why do hot things always cool down?' Boltzmann hanged himself aged 62, while his wife and daughters went to the sea to bathe on a warm September evening in Duino, Italy. He said he would follow them down to the bay, but when his daughter went back to check on him, she found him hanging by the window frame in the seaside hotel.

Now, Boltzmann loved Beethoven.

Always craving recognition, Botlzmann was desperate for acceptance and yet terrified of the change that would take him to where he needed to be. He was paralysed by a fear of what others thought of him. As a dinner guest at the home of a respected professor, he picked up the wrong piece of cutlery, and was told by the Professor's wife: 'Herr Boltzmann, in Berlin you will not fit in.'

He could never forget it.

After rushing to capture the visions of his mathematics, Boltzmann did not go back to correct or neaten up his theories. Elegance is for tailors, he told his students. The energy, the passion, the *sturm und drang* was everything.

Yes, Boltzmann loved Beethoven. Music that sounds like self-sabotage. Music that is better for the extremes.

In the second movement of Beethoven's 7th Symphony, you get close to feeling, perhaps as best you can, what another person might feel when their life dedicated to a single question hasn't given the answer they needed, and rather than join their wife and daughters by the sea on a summer evening, they hang themselves in a hotel room.

It is said of Beethoven's *Appassionata*, that one hand asks questions that the other hand answers. Or chooses not to. Milan Kundera references this in *The Unbearable Lightness of Being*. In the last movement of Beethoven's last quartet, the left hand asks:

Muss es sein? Must it be?

The right hand answers:

Es muss sein! It must be!

And Tomas knows he must go to the woman he is falling in love with.

'*Ja, es muss sein!* Tomas said again.'

Geoff Dyer writes of moments in life of *bejahung*, which can be translated as 'yes-ing'; giving a fundamental yes to life, knowing in an instant with absolute certainty what must be done.

With the piano sonatas, Beethoven's technique is to leave a dominant harmony hanging, unresolved. In this way, questions come, and keep coming, and go unanswered. And in the final movement there is an emphatic fulfilment, a resounding resolution as all the questions are answered at once.

Elegance is for tailors, he told his students. The energy, the passion, the *sturm und drang* was everything

I stayed once in a seaside hotel in Tenby. There was a large square coffee-table book of Buddhist quotations, written in italic script over supposedly profound photos, such as a raindrop on a rose petal, or an autumn leaf in a doorway; you know the kind of thing. I read this quote: 'If you keep asking the same question, you will get the same answer'. It sounded, well, profound.

What is the question we should be asking?

—

For hundreds of years my dad's ancestors toiled the East Anglian soil. They are recorded as Ag Lab – meaning Agricultural Labourer – in the parish records that date back to the 1600s. They are buried in graveyards across Norfolk, in most cases within a mile of where they were born. My grandad Victor left school at 14 and cycled from farm to farm, asking for work. His father died before he was born and he saw his mother a couple of times a year. She worked in service in hotels across the country. In the middle of the chaffing, and the thatching, and the yelming, he was sent to war. He was 21.

My grandfather patted him on the shoulder in comradery, and the man fell down dead in front of him

Over 338,000 Allied soldiers were evacuated between the 27th of May and the 4th of June 1940 at Dunkirk. Yet the Norfolk Regiment was ordered to march *towards* the approaching Nazi army to help hold back the advance, and buy more time for the evacuation. Eventually the regiment was told to head for Saint Valery-en-Caux for their rescue. Strategically, it was one of the worst possible places for an evacuation, a small harbour town with little space for mooring. Following days of artillery fire, the entire town was ablaze. At 3am on the 12th of June, my grandad walked along the sand, bodies rolling back and forth in the waves at the shoreline. He met a solider from the Royal Indian Army Service Corps who said, 'Hello, old chap'. My grandad patted him on the shoulder in comradery, and the man fell down dead in front of him. Overhead Stukas, fitted with a siren deliberately designed to cause panic, nose-dived almost vertically. My grandad, who had by then been told that no further evacuation was possible, and that it was 'every man for himself', made it out into the black of the sea in a fishing boat, rowing with a shovel.

He was picked up by the Navy, and the next morning they docked in Plymouth. He celebrated with an ice cream. The first of his life.

Because he escaped, he was able to have a son, my dad.

Perhaps it seemed my dad would join the long line of *Ag Labs*. He grew up in a council house in a rural Norfolk village and went to the local Secondary Modern. Yet fuelled by a mother 'who loved him without limit and without question' – he wrote many years later for her funeral – he made it to Central London Poly to study Astrophysics. During his long career in space science he designed one of 12 instruments that landed on a comet, launched from Rosetta, to examine whether water, and therefore life, originated on comets.

Nullius in Verba: take nobody's word for it. As a child my dad told me to always remember the motto of the Royal Society; that nobody has authority just because of who they are. I wish my grandad had known this when Captain *Oxfordschnösel* patted him on the back saying 'good boys the Norfolk-ies' as he marched towards the Nazi gunfire, so that the captain could march towards his rescue.

I remember prototype models of spacecraft parts – Solar Max, Atlantis, ROSAT – sitting in our kitchen as Dad enthused over the design. He worked on projects that would yield results long after he had retired. Many scientists dedicate their life to a small, specialised area; one question that may turn out to be entirely the wrong thread, and yet they contribute to knowledge because they usefully close off a dead end.

The poet Rabindranath Tagore, who incidentally corresponded with Einstein in the 1930s, wrote:

'The one who plants trees, knowing that he will never sit in their shade, has at least started to understand the meaning of life.'

—

As a species, we've got it all wrong, picked up the wrong thread, told the wrong story. And now our story is coming to an end. *Muss es sein?* But to end the story for all life? Now that would be a very unhappy ending indeed. And so with urgency, with *sturm und drang*, we need to start telling the only story that matters.

—

In the observable universe there are 30,000,000,000,000,000,000,000 billion stars like our sun. Most of them have planets orbiting them. I don't know how to feel, or even say this number. To try to grasp it, I first try to really understand the scale of just one million. I search visual representations of a million, and find this picture of a million dots on a page:

It doesn't help much.

If you want to see what a billion dots looks like there is a film on YouTube of dots repeating in grids of 10,000. It takes two hours and 39 minutes to watch; just to see one billion. Of course, it is impossible to feel the reality of 30,000,000,000,000,000,000,000 billion stars.

There is an absence.

What would it even mean to be able to imagine this number?

———

In a short breath we have come close to destroying the entire ecology of our little planet.

Is conscious life worth preserving?

Is it an evolutionary mistake?

Are we worth saving?

Perhaps not.

But what about all that beautiful less-conscious life that enjoys the sun on its back without questioning why, without needing to write a story that could have been better. Now that life, is that worth saving?

B E J A H U N G!

And perhaps also a species that can put the *Appassionata* into the universe?

B E J A H U N G!

And a species that can land a space probe on a comet 300 million miles from Earth?

B E J A H U N G!

To save this little planet from ourselves we are going to need to a very good story indeed.

In the beginning there was…

Bacteria and archaea, clustered around hydrothermal vents in the ocean.

And just once in the entire 4.5 billion years of planet Earth, and, as far as is known just once in the entire universe of planets orbiting 30,000,000,000,000,000,000,000,000 billion stars;

Something happened.

A bacteria was absorbed by archaea and it produced a eukaryote, and this moment gave rise to every living thing in the known universe.

Everything from an incident so rare, it has happened only once, as far as is known, anywhere in the universe, in 13.8 billion years. The moment that gave rise to all life happened just once, which is why of course we share 99% of our DNA with chimpanzees and bonobos, and 70% with oak trees. Never mind the difference between a Republican and a Democrat, a Brexiteer and a Remainer, or an Arab and a Jew; we're not all that different from wood.

I am the tree that trembles and trembles

Anyway, the brief point I wanted to make was that the poem about the cunts and the penises is brilliant. It stops me midway through.

I am working out the vocabulary of my silence.

Einstein didn't speak until he was three, and when he could speak he had worked out the vocabulary of silence; that to understand is to see not speak. He changed the course of human history by seeing that the gravitational field is not diffused through space; the gravitational field is that space itself. And then he worked out the maths to prove it.

Even a *Physics for Beginners* book assumes you know what calculus is, yet with a God the story is often very simple, and very easy to pass on.

Mary. Carpenter. Donkey. Star. Rat a tat tat. Baby. Myrrh. Shepherds.

Lepers. Prostitutes. Fish. Loaves. Last supper. Cross. Cave. Easter Eggs.

The universe is made of atoms, but the only animal that knows this thinks mostly in stories.

What story would tell the rarity of life, as beautifully as the story of a young couple starting out on a journey together, having a baby, and getting some odd presents from kind visitors? All under the brightest star.

What story could unite us enough to save the only known instance of life in the universe?

The poem about the atoms and stories, the cunts and penises is so brilliant, because it knows that it's about capturing the story that is bigger than us, and bigger that the single act of becoming a mother or father.

> *Life the announcer.*
> *I assure you*
> *there are many ways to have a child.*
> *I bastard mother*
> *promise you*
> *there are many ways to be born.*
> *They all come forth*
> *in their own grace.*

There are many ways to have a child. Planting seeds. Telling the true story.

And oh how the poem ends, the weight of how it ends:

Who will speak these days,
if not I,
if not you? ◨

Bibliography

Al-Khalili, Jim and McFadden, Johnjoe. *Life on the Edge. The Coming of Age of Quantum Biology*. Penguin Random House (2014)

Barenboim, Daniel. *Everything is Connected*. Phoenix (2009)

Dyer, Geoff. *Out of Sheer Rage*. Abacus (1998)

Lindley, David. *Boltzmann's Atom*. The Free Press (2001)

Lockwood, Lewis. *Beethoven: The Music and the Life*. Norton (2005)

Rovelli, Carlo. *Reality is Not What it Seems*. Penguin Random House (2017)

Rukeyser, Muriel. *Out of Silence: Selected Poems*. TriQuarterly Books (1992)

Tagore, Rabrindranath. *The Essential Tagore*. Harvard University Press (2011)

The Royal Society of Literature

JOIN US

With our Autumn/Winter '21 events programme, there's never been a better time to become a Member of the Royal Society of Literature.

As an RSL Member, you'll get:

- Free tickets to in-person and online events
- Our quarterly newspaper, *Our Mutual Friend*
- A free subscription to the annual *RSL Review* magazine
- Special offers from our wonderful partners across theatre, film and all things literary

All of this could be yours, with Membership starting at just £40 for a whole year.

With Christmas just around the corner, give the gift of literature with an RSL Gift Membership!

Wherever you are, be part of the action by snapping up an RSL Digital Events Pass today! Our entire season is available online for just £25 a year so you won't miss a thing.

Recent and forthcoming speakers **include:**

Gwen Adshead, **Charlie Jane Anders,** Lisa Appignanesi,
Carole Angier, Shahida Bari, **Lucy Caldwell,**
Steve Cavanagh, **Michael Dirda,** Merve Emre, **Brian Eno,**
Stephen Fry, **Neil Gaiman,** Salena Godden,
David Harewood, Pico Iyer, **Marlon James,**
Shaparak Khorsandi, **Patrice Lawrence,** CN Lester,
Deborah Levy, Val McDermid, **Ian McDonald,** David
Mitchell, **Sarah Moss,** Joyce Carol Oates, **Irenosen
Okojie,** Abby Oliveira, **Ruth Padel,** Michael Palin, **Glenn
Patterson,** Claudia Rankine, **Chris Riddell,** Iain
Sinclair, **Colin Thubron,** Jack Underwood, **Kit de Waal,**
Alex Wheatle, **Gary Younge** & Máire Zepf.

JOIN NOW

Gator Love

by Pune Dracker

From Whence It Came Is Mystery

So said *The New York Times*, February 9, 1935,
regarding an eight-foot, 125-pound alligator
found in a sewer on 123rd Street. A group of teens
discovered the reptile while shoveling snow into a
manhole, and used a clothesline as a noose to drag
him out. Their 'curiosity and sympathy turned to
enmity,' however, when they removed the rope and
the gator snapped at them.

'Let 'im have it!' the boys cried,
and pummeled the alligator to death with their shovels.

And here we all thought it was an urban legend,
like in the movie Alligator, where a 36-foot mutant
gator goes around murdering cops and reporters.

The thing about fiction is that sometimes it is not.
While it wasn't unusual for reporters at the time
to embellish their stories, a number of other area
papers ran similar accounts. It was posited that a)
the Uptown Sewer Alligator had hitched a ride on
a steamer from the Everglades, or b) he could have
been someone's pet gone wild. Back then, anyone
could purchase a baby alligator by mail order, for
$1.50, postpaid.

> *Think of the fun, the thrills you will have*
> read an ad in Popular Mechanics.
> *Do you want a Baby Alligator? You bet you do.*

—

Unlike alligators, snakes do not have two sets – not
even one set! – of eyelids
Unlike alligators, snakes do not have limbs
Unlike alligators, snakes live up to their urban legends.

The Limelight Nightclub opened in 1983 on
20th Street and Avenue of the Americas, in the
former home of the Episcopal Church of the Holy
Communion. It is not easy for a church to become
a dance floor – it first has to be deconsecrated, a
service whereby a sacred space is made suitable for
secular use. Consecrated objects are removed, and
the Declaration of Secularization, revoking the
sentence of consecration, is read.

I cannot say if snakes or alligators ever went to the Episcopal Church of the Holy Communion, but there were snakes at The Limelight. I know because I brought one there. It was around the year 2000, and my friend Mike called to ask if I could participate in his art installation that evening, to be held in the part of the club where the chapel would have been when it was a church. He asked me to portray the Virgin Mary and said I should define the role myself, so I brought a red-tailed boa constrictor named Girlsnake. I also brought her favorite climbing branch, more like a climbing bush strung with tiny white flowers, and placed it in front of a small platform. I was wearing a black dress, rosary beads and no shoes. 'Stand there for 15 minutes,' Mike said. I was surprised by how easy it was to remain completely still. After an hour, with Girlsnake lacing and relacing herself through my fingers, I heard people debating whether or not I was real.

'Look at the feet, though,' they said. 'They're too white.' And,
'Ewwww, a snake.'

> If science deconsecrates, fiction is consecrating.
> Most
> people would
>> say, I would say, that a sewer has always
>> been secular.

―

The large and intimidating mother provides most of their protection:
Knowing that alligators exhibit an incredible degree of parental care – they guard their eggs like birds, scoop the hatchlings into their mouths and escort them to the water, where they stand guard against predators for months, even a year – I want to write a letter to Uptown Sewer Alligator's mother.

I want to tell her I am sorry her son's life ended in the manner it did, but that he is epochal. That there is a day celebrated in his honor. Alligators in the Sewer Day, every February 9.

—

Meditation # 1
In New York City, the greatest city on earth, where one Uptown Sewer Alligator is not enough, we pledge our allegiance to belief in an eternally proliferating colony of sightless, albino alligators, deformed from living in a sluice of toxic waste. Bigger, so big, from feasting on garbage and rabid rats.

The thing about fiction is that sometimes it is.

—

Shortly before hatching, baby alligators – still inside their eggs – begin calling for their mothers, singing baby alligator songs.

> Sewer gator songs sound of gush and suck,
> of rumble and smack and somewhere
> a place for us

Meditation #2

a) Anything can happen in a fictional world.

b) Because anything can happen in a fictional world, a fictional world could be constructed of people and ideas and actions that all are perfect.

c) Even when things that happen in a fictional world are not perfect, they can potentially turn perfect because a) & b)

d) In a perfect world, the Uptown Sewer Alligator does not get lassoed and bludgeoned to death by boys with shovels. In a perfect world, he is accepted for who he is, lives free from harm and stars in a short play, in which he portrays himself.

———

Question: Is New York City the only city a) known for having/not having alligators in the sewers and b) killing them?

In Paris, sewer workers found a little crocodile under the Pont Neuf Bridge in 1984. They rescued her, christened her Eleanore and brought her to the Paris Zoo. Eleanore is still alive and living in an aquarium in Vannes, on the southern coast of Brittany, eating *un poulet* a week.

———

Gator Love: a play

Scene: An apartment in Brooklyn Heights, 11 pm.
Starring: GATOR'S MOM and GATOR

GATOR'S MOM: Gator, time for bed!
GATOR: Last one in's a rotten one![1]

GATOR'S MOM and GATOR race each other to
the bedroom. GATOR'S MOM jumps into bed as
GATOR climbs a gator-sized set of steps and crawls
into bed. GATOR'S MOM rearranges the blankets
as GATOR snuggles under the covers and puts his
head on GATOR'S MOM's chest.

GATOR: I wuv you![2]

GATOR does not say but is thinking *Around here,
every day is Alligators in the Sewer Day.*
GATOR does not say but is thinking *Now I know
another love song.*

---

1 The science is that alligators chirp, hiss, rumble and bellow, thanks to their human-
anatomy-like larynx and vocal folds, and a muscle called the glottal adductor that
affords them a high level of vocal control. The fiction is that a) alligators have not been
recorded mimicking human speech, and b) GATOR sounds like Mishka, the talking
Siberian husky who could say 12 words, including 'Obama' and 'Hello.'

2 The science is that alligators don't have facial muscles, so they can't smile even
if smiles mean to alligators what they mean to people. The fiction are the words
GATOR uses to expresses his contentment. Does GATOR really know what 'wuv' is?

In this life you can pack and ship many things, but not *Uromastyx aegyptia*. Years ago, I cared for three wild-caught spiny tailed lizards who were seized at JFK Airport. Someone had stolen them from their Middle Eastern home, piled them in a cardboard box on top of dozens of other lizards, and shipped them to America for the exotic pet trade. We were to hold them while a court case was pending; the uromastyx lizards were weak and sick from the journey, so it was more like hospice.

I marveled at their soft pebble-gray skin, dinosaur heads, spiked tails, kind eyes… they spent most of the time still, like ectothermic Romanesque cathedrals. Despite my best efforts, first little Memphis passed away, then Lotus. Gaza was cracker-thin but still ate her alfalfa hay every day. I hired an animal communicator to check in with her, and Gaza told the animal communicator she was so tired. And she *just wanted to go home*.

My heart fell. She could never go back – we didn't even know where home was – and I knew deep down that a 75-gallon tank with full-spectrum lighting and a bunch of heat lamps in an East Village apartment was so, so wrong. When she passed, I imagined her dreaming herself back to soft, silken sand near the hottest rocks she could find. Sunlight so blinding it could penetrate the sewer she had found herself in, the sewer that was the entirety of New York City.

Q. Three reasons why we need to believe there are giant mutant alligators in New York City sewers

Something in us albino and mutant
Something in us afraid of milk or hair
Something in us murderous

—

It is hard for us, in our bubble of select-quantity-color-and-size-from-the-drop-down-menu, to believe that something, someone could be one of a kind. The Uptown Sewer Alligator was just that. Biologists will tell you: quite simply, it is too cold for alligators to live in New York City sewers. They need warmth to digest food, and if they did eat anything, the food would rot inside, causing them to perish. The pollution levels do not allow life, any life. You can ask the former reptile keeper at the Staten Island Zoo, who, as a kid, spent the summer his street was under construction 'fishing' in the sewer for gators. He didn't catch any.

—

A. Open Letter to Uptown Sewer Alligator's Mother

Dear Mom,
Your freewheeling son gives us a safe place to stow our horror, our filthy giggles.
We are still talking about him. ◨

£35
FULL SET

boilerhouse.press

EWAN FERNIE & SIMON PALFREY   **STEVE HAN**

OUT { "MACBETH, MACBETH," A SHAKEN BIBLE TEXTUAL NON SENSE THE SICK LIST

NOW

BEYOND CRITICISM EDITION

ROBERT CRAWFORD   **ANSGAR AL**

BOILER

HOUSE

PRESS

NEW FORMS FOR NEW THINKING ABOUT LITERATURE

"A glorious, shimmering and strange collection."

NEW FICTION

AM I IN THE RIGHT PLACE?
BEN PESTER

boilerhouse.press

BOILER
HOUSE
PRESS

– Irenosen Okojie, author of *Nudibranch*

Birds

by Chris Cusack

The only acceptable excuse for not having a bird feeder
in the back garden [is having] one in the front garden.
– Rónán Hession, *Leonard and Hungry Paul*

I have convinced myself that songbirds will only successfully establish
themselves in gardens they recognise from collective memory –
gardens their ancestors frequented in generations past.
– Sara Baume, *handiwork*

The birds were always there.
– Richard Smyth, *An Indifference of Birds*

i. Waders

Perhaps my love for lines and patterns derives from
the fact that I spent part of my childhood in the
400-year-old Beemster polder in the Netherlands,
a mesh of pastures and tulip fields crisscrossed with
roads and canals and girded by miles of dikes.
A postcard scene, pinned into place by trees and
houses and windmills, and by the spires of the two
main churches – one Catholic, one Protestant –
jutting imperiously into the boundless sky.

Everything I look at – landscape, text, set of
random objects – instantly organises itself, or
is organised by me, into parallels and tangents,
intersections and symmetries, curves and angles.
The patterns I detect or seek to create aren't
necessarily geometrically perfect: I'm often
delighted by details in paintings or landscapes that

randomly break order. It's not really about imposing a sense of regularity on an otherwise chaotic world, but rather about the intrinsic beauty of patterning, the way the rhythm of repetition and variation produces a melody of the visual.

Most nature in the Netherlands, even in areas formally designated as 'wild', is carefully managed, but while it is easy enough to lose sight of this fact when you go off-track in the forest, the grid pattern of the Beemster polder precludes such denial of human design. And yet the polder has a unique ecosystem, with an impressive diversity of fauna. The cows and sheep, of course, betoken human settlement and industry, while the canals – sticklebacks, bass, bream and, long ago, an abundance of eels – are much less controlled.

The fields do not only harbour lifestock, though. They are also the domain of leporids, muskrats (nemesis of dikereeves), shrews, and voles, and endless numbers of insects. Agitating the soil, there's a whole economy of moles, bugs, earthworms. The polder is essentially an all-you-can-eat buffet, and it's not surprising that buzzards and kites and sparrowhawks are a common sight.

Yet as much as I admire the insouciant ruthlessness of these raptors, the thing that has always appealed to me most in the Beemster is the avian life thriving on the very edges of the fields and holding dominion in the canals: the many types of wading and aquatic birds, some common, some rare, that found their ideal habitat in this touchstone of early modern civil engineering.

There's an abundance of grey herons, and over the past decades storks have become increasingly common. Ducks and coots and lapwings are everywhere, and twice a year the polder is taken over by huge flocks of migrating geese, whose honking punctuates the days and nights for weeks.

These are only the more common residents, however. The Beemster is particularly renowned for its population of rare or seasonal wading birds, including snipes, curlews with their splendidly customised bills, and the Dutch national bird, the black-tailed godwit, whose name in Dutch is the onomatopoeic *grutto*, after its highly recognisable call: Utto! Utto! Utto!

One morning we woke up to find the field next to our house full of common spoonbills, dozens of them. Spoonbills are strange creatures. With their white plumage, long black legs, weird mullet, and that long black bill which broadens at the end into yellow castanets, they look like the result of a boozy tryst between a swan, a stork, and a cockatoo. Though apparently they're not particularly rare in the Netherlands, we'd never seen a colony this large. By the time we got home from school that afternoon they'd flown.

I have five siblings. Between the eldest and the youngest of us, there's a mere decade. We all have an astonishing capacity for talk, as well as an astonishing interest in just about anything that crosses our paths. To ferry this parliament of Cusacks around the polder, my parents bought a tiny Subaru minivan that could just about hold six slightly built children in the back and, in front, two average-sized adults. The Subaru was almost taller than it was long, and every time a milk truck passed us on its way to the Beemster cheese factory, we would rock from side to side, and our mother's hands would clench the wheel lest vehicle and chattering cargo tumble into the canal.

While my mother is technically a both-hands-on-the-wheel-at-all-times driver, she'll often abandon this rule to point out some bird flapping overhead or perched on a fence or half-hidden in a tree. Indeed, though my parents have never been real birders in the sense that they won't lie in ambush in a bog to spot birds, they always have a pair of binoculars beneath the driver's seat and a birding guide in the glove compartment. I think this started in the Beemster. We'd be driving around the polder, and suddenly my mother would swerve into a lay-by or a bus stop or sometimes simply the grass verge, swoop the binos out of their case, and point out a distant bird with a delighted index finger.

If she didn't immediately recognise her target, the guide would come out and we'd try to determine the species, a challenge that often continued after we'd resumed our journey. Whoever was in the passenger seat had to read out the descriptions of the birds she named and we'd deliberate about whether or not that was the one we'd spotted. Once, we ID'ed an ibis this way; it must've strayed pretty far from its original course.

—

Years later, we moved to a village in the rural south of the Netherlands. Heeswijk isn't a polder, and the south-east of the country has a very different smell from the north-west. The sky, too, is different, has finite proportions. It partly makes up for these differences with a fine range of trees, but for a long time it didn't feel quite like home.

Here too, though, we found a riches of birds, albeit different ones. No godwits or spoonbills or curlews, but a broader range of raptors, a compendium of robins and thrushes and tits, pheasants, more owls than you could shake a stick at. One year a common kingfisher nested by the stream running directly behind our house, and we'd sometimes see it flitting across the water, a blue-and-amber blur so swift it seemed to mock our desire to recognise it.

There was also one summer when every day around 6am two green woodpeckers would dash to and fro overhead as I slouched groggily to my job at the hotel a few minutes down the road, their aerobatics momentarily distracting me from the lure of that vital first cappuccino.

ii. Owls

I have a beautiful blue quilt that reminds me of the polder, with its subdivision of squares and its splendid lines. It was hand-stitched for me by my Dutch grandmother, Oma, who made, I think, about thirty in total: a quilt each for every child and grandchild, and several more for other relatives and friends, all tailored to their specific tastes.

Mine, though, was the first that had her signature stitched into it, several squares with owls on them. Oma had a fondness for the strigine and had amassed a large display of owl objects. We briefly considered giving every mourner at her funeral one of her figurines as a memento, but instead decided to box them up until one of the grandchildren has enough space to reinstate the full collection.

Oma had a fondness for the strigine and had amassed a large display of owl objects

Oma and my grandfather, Oudje, lived with us in the Beemster, first in the massive old convent my parents had bought and then in the old farmhouse we rented after the company my father worked for had been forced to downsize and my parents could no longer afford the mortgage.

Though the owls were Oma's thing, Oudje was the naturalist of the two. Following early retirement, he spent most of his time outside in our massive garden, tending the fruit trees and his vegetable patch, cutting down trees, and generally just pottering about, thinking about gooseberries and the meaning of life.

After school, we'd join him, and we'd meander between the many topics encompassed by his remarkable sense of curiosity. Most days, he'd talk about the garden (not *qua* garden but qua phenomenon), point out the patterning on a leaf or the way a particular tree branched out, pick up a newt for us to hold and feel the coolness of its skin and the slither of its quicksilver body, or he'd dig up from the pockets of his overalls some pebble he'd found with a strange shape or pretty sheen.

Having grown up in Amsterdam during the Second World War, his embrace of nature and rejection of the urban was perhaps deeper than we were inclined to think

It was Oudje in particular who made the natural world part of our everyday experience and vocabulary. Having grown up in Amsterdam during the Second World War, his embrace of nature and rejection of the urban was perhaps deeper than we were inclined to think. When his dementia worsened, the memories that persisted longest were urban, and not the nice ones, but his desire to go into the outdoors survived much longer than his ability to articulate his thoughts, to the extent that we had to lock the doors to prevent him from disappearing into the fields.

Though my parents conceived of birds as visual objects first and foremost, for Oudje they were ephemeral sounds as much as material phenomena, and he'd often try to teach us to recognise their calls. With Oma or him, we'd often sing a well-known Dutch children's song about golden orioles [*wielewaal*; cf. Middle English *woodwele*], to be sung in canon, a great genre if you need to entertain a horde of grandchildren: a half-dozen voices belting out *kom NUUU naar BUUUI-ten AAA-llemaal, dan ZOE-ken WIJ de WIEHIEHIE-le-WAAL* – 'now come outside all of you, and we'll go look for the oriole'.

But the hooting of an owl was his favourite sound to share with his grandchildren. He'd fold his big mitts around our hands, gently bend our fingers with his, and then call like an owl into the echo chamber thus created: OO-hoo! OO-hoo! OO-hoo!

—

Across the road from my flat is the depot of the local museum of natural history. The most spectacular objects, of course, are part of the museum's main exhibition – my own favourite, and no doubt that of most, is the mammoth skull found in a nearby gravel pit – but here they keep the thousands of specimens that might be of scientific or historical interest but aren't exciting enough to be on permanent display.

A friend of mine used to work there, and she gave me a tour of the vault once, where these specimens, taxidermied or otherwise preserved, are carefully stored. Seeing so many individuals of different species frozen in time was a strange, disorienting experience. Shelves and shelves of hedgehogs, rats, badgers, rabbits, all in slightly different positions, and none moving even a whisker. Not a zoo but a hallucination. But my favourite was the cabinet full of local owls staring down death with identical glass eyes. Barn owls, little owls, and long-eared owls mostly.

Like my grandmother, the museum collected owls, but while Oma was interested in gathering as wide a range of objects as possible, the Natuurmuseum needed to have a representative sample of local fauna rather than an aficionado's collection. Not scores of objects in a range of materials and guises, but multiple biological specimens of the same species, whose variations in this hidden wunderkammer were examples of taxidermic artistry rather than expressions of creative license or avian individuality.

iii. Raptors, etc.

I'm not actually much of a nature writer, to be honest. My capacity for the sort of description that typifies the best examples of the genre is limited, and I find it challenging to compile lists of names and generi that are as poetic as they are informative. What's worse: so far, I've had to look up the names for about half the birds I've mentioned. They don't come to mind effortlessly.

My engagement with the avian world, and indeed the environment more generally, is almost exclusively codified in Dutch. The landscapes I've inhabited are contoured in its diphthongs and gutturals. Oudje talked about birds in Dutch; the birding guide we consulted with our mother was written in Dutch. The signs in the zoos we visited were in Dutch.

If I want to discuss birds or plants or trees in another tongue, even English, my brain dishes up the source material in Dutch. But though I *feel* nature in Dutch, for me the act of writing in general only feels instinctive in English. My language somehow feels more versatile and sinuous, is quicker to take flight. Whenever I write in Dutch, it feels as if I'm lagging behind my own thoughts. As such, when I try to write about nature, I find myself obliged to pummel my thoughts into a shape that differs frustratingly from their original presentation.

If I want to discuss birds or plants or trees in another tongue, even English, my brain dishes up the source material in Dutch

The degree of constructedness is no different in English or Dutch, of course, and writing's a slog in whatever language you use. But even though Dutch, technically, is my first language, I feel removed somehow from the reality I'm trying to construct. It's a different kind of struggle than writing in English, rather as if I'm forced to perform a rough simulacrum of the act of composition.

In a sense, I'm suspended between languages; my dominant tongue is no longer the one that gave shape to these experiences I'm trying to describe. But if language and experience are thus intertwined, can I actually claim to know nature at all? Am I writing about birds, or only ever about language?

Growing up, I think the only bird whose name I first learned in English was the red kite. My uncle and aunt live in England, in the Chilterns, close to the woods. The area is full of these magnificent fork-tailed raptors, and whenever we visit, my parents cannot hide their joy at spotting so many of them circling overhead. I particularly like sitting in the conservatory at the back of the house; usually, you can see several gliding through the air at the same time, and if the French doors to the garden are open, you'll hear their shrill, imperious calls.

iv. Passerines
In the Netherlands, languages are a central part of the secondary school curriculum. At the gymnasium, the highest level, students have to study six languages: four living, two dead. While we hardly went beyond generic names for plants and animals in six years of English and French and five years of German – butterfly, papillon, Schmetterling – in the classical languages we had to be much more specific in our determinations.

I don't envy the teachers who had to do Catullus 16 with a cohort of sixteen-year-olds, and explain its highly graphic opening line

For Latin, the central author in Year 4 was Catullus, and we spent all year analysing and translating his work. Not just the more *salonfähige* poems about love and grief, but also some of his NSFW stuff. I don't envy the teachers who had to do Catullus 16 with a cohort of sixteen-year-olds, and explain its highly graphic opening line, 'Pedicabo ego vos et irrumabo' – a bit rude even in Peter Green's sanitised translation: 'Up yours both, and sucks to the pair of you'.

The first poem we translated was 2A, one of the poet's more lovey-dovey poems addressed to 'Lesbia' or Clodia. It begins with the name of a bird: 'Passer, deliciae meae puellae' – 'sparrow, precious darling of my sweetheart', in Green's version. The Dutch key gave the translation 'musje', the diminutive of 'mus', sparrow. The diminutive, though not explicit in Latin, is presumably a metrical choice. However, our teacher took a good ten minutes to argue why 'mus' itself made little sense in this context, explaining that the bird most commonly referred to in Dutch by this generic name would likely not have been the kind Clodia owned.

But this meant that this bird, which I could recognise only in translation, was actually not the one I thought it was based on this crude but functional interpretation. And this was before my teacher started outlining the subtexts of Catullus' sparrow, which is often read as a phallic symbol, a reading that further complicates the simple translation 'musje', metrically and idiomatically correct though it might seem. This explanation seemed far-fetched initially, but browsing through my recently purchased Latin-English bilingual edition, I'm struck by how obvious many of Catullus' innuendos actually are. I suppose we were too distracted by the highly explicit nature of some of the other poems to notice the more subtle references to sins of the flesh.

The writer central to the national curriculum in the year of my finals was Ovid, mainly *Metamorphoses* and, if I remember correctly, parts of *Ars Amatoria*. The former is full of birds, including the infamous story of sisters Philomela and Procne, and the violent King Tereus, Procne's husband. This is one of Ovid's most monstrous tales, and it ends with the transformation of the main characters into birds. The description of the sisters' metamorphosis seems purposely designed to torture bored teens forced to translate its contortions: 'Corpora Cecropidum pennis pendere putares: / pendebant pennis.'

The onomatopoeic repetition of the plosives c, p, d, and t mimics the flapping of wings, a typically Ovidian effect, as is the chiasmus at the end, syntax mirroring transformation. Frank Justus Miller's Loeb translation isn't quite as elegant, though its alliterative fricatives have a similar vibe, as does the repetition at the end (even if it's not chiastic): 'As they fly from him you would think that the bodies of the two Athenians were poised on wings: they were poised on wings!'

Like many poets I've always been particularly interested in poor Icarus, not least because of the various layerings that have defined my understanding of the myth. There's the painting by (or attributed to) Bruegel; the ekphrastic meditations on this work by William Carlos Williams and W.H. Auden; the episode of the 1990s miniseries *The Storyteller: Greek Myths*; and my own tentative engagements with Ovid's original, as well as the English translations I've been reading.

My youthful determination to parlay the myth into a metaphor for my own condition as a writer, however, was obviously an embarrassing cliché. And yet: the affectation that was casting myself as a creature of verse and hubris, as a *poète maudit* who must write but could claim no language, no element as his own and is thus destroyed, made Icarus a convenient symbol. After all, the story of Icarus isn't really about the fall or about hubris, I think. He is not the problem, but the failure of the artifice, when the wax and feathers, the paperclips and sellotape and bits of string, the chewed-up pencil, can no longer sustain the exigencies of fabrication and metaphor.

The most interesting elements of Ovid's account for me, though, aren't Icarus' fall and metamorphosis, but the moments before that, particularly the father's passing transformation as he teaches his son to fly. In Arthur Golding's 1567 translation, Daedalus isn't a bird but a simile. He's like a bird, and this only for the duration of a scant few lines:

> And then he mounting up aloft before him
> tooke his way
> Right fearfull for his followers sake: as is the
> Bird the day
> That first she tolleth from hir nest among
> the braunches hie
> Hir tender yong ones in the Aire to teach
> them for to flie.

While father and son soar through the sky, Ovid firmly plants us on terra firma. And here we have that famous scene: Bruegel, Auden – but also, yes, the Beemster. Lines cast into the water, lines cast to the ground, lines ploughed into the fields. The screeching of gulls.

> The fishermen
> Then standing angling by the Sea, and
> shepeherdes leaning then
> On sheepehookes, and the Ploughmen on
> the handles of their Plough,
> Beholding them, amazed were: and thought
> that they that through
> The Aire could flie were Gods.

Here, then, I find myself. Because these, you see, are no gods, no birds, but mere souls: just humans, and their desire to find the words for flight. ∎

LONDON LIT LAB

Online courses in 2022, for beginner to advanced writers:

- Creative Nonfiction: Compelling Memoir
- Saltwater Folk Tales
- Therapeutic Writing: Trauma-informed Foundation Programme
- Short Story Gold Rush: Write your Way to the Treasure
- How to Write a Compelling Memoir Proposal
- Short Story Bootcamp: Fix, Polish, Submit!
- and many more!

Or join a **Live Online** masterclass, including:

- How to Pitch your Writing with agent Ben Dunn
- Writing our Many Queer Stories with Andrew Kaufmann

Join our community and nurture your talent in a supportive environment with like-minded people, where writers teach writers.

'Lily and Zoe offer teaching and coaching at the highest level. Their workshops have a reputation for encouraging excellence and creativity in a supportive environment. I am always recommending them.' Julia Bell, Course Convenor, MA Creative Writing, Birkbeck.

www.londonlitlab.co.uk

The Shapeshifters

by Carla Montemayor

When my body becomes water
My form turns to liquid
Don't neglect me
Don't ignore me
Don't lose a single drop
Of my body
            – Matan-ayon to her husband Sinagnayan,
               in a verse from the epic *Derikaryong Pada*

I suppose I should start with a few facts. That way, this tale resembles your idea of a history. A collection of facts told in an approved sequence and recorded in script.

My aunt's name was Fe. She was born in 1946 in the north-east of the Philippines, as the country pieced itself together from the three-year savaging of the Second World War. The youngest of seven siblings, she had two sisters, my mother being the eldest. She was an anthropologist, a feminist, a teacher. She raised two sons. What can you glean from this information that is of any interest to you?

Let me begin instead with an afternoon a few Octobers ago when a sandstorm turned the London sky carnelian. Stripes of terror lined my aunt's forehead as we stood in Trafalgar Square. She was almost 71, retired and travelling to countries where her sons and nieces could distract her from digging in the rubble of her recent widowhood.

It's just Hurricane Ophelia, I assured her, after checking the news. My aunt and I had lived through numerous disasters in the tropics, surely dust blowing in from the Sahara was a distant threat.

She started weeping. My late mother was called Ofelia. In naming the hurricane, I had invoked her sister.

—

> *They are so ignorant that they do not have*
> *the slightest knowledge concerning the origin*
> *of the ancestors from whom they descend,*
> *and whence they came to settle these islands.*
> — Gaspar de San Agustín,
> Augustinian missionary, *The Philippine Islands,*
> *1493-1898* - Volume 40 of 55 (1690-1691)

My mother's sisters were born in the north, as was their father, but their mother was from the island of Panay in the central cluster of the Philippine archipelago. They were specifically from Aklan, one of its four provinces. I was well into adulthood when I heard of an anthropologist called F. Landa Jocano and his pioneering research in the region, never suspecting it had any connection to me or my family. In 1955, he travelled among mountain villages recording folk stories, proverbs and poems. Local folk told him of the Hinilawod, a tale recited by elders on special occasions.

Halawod (Jalaur on contemporary maps) is a river in Panay, the Hinilawod a collection of sung poems issuing from the people of the Halawod.

Jocano would find an elderly woman, Hugan-an, who could recite the Hinilawod's three chapters. Hugan-an had been a binukot: a woman secluded in her girlhood, kept away from the sun and the eyes of village folk, exempted from all work. Her task was to remember her people's stories.

—

> *On some summer nights, I joined my uncle's family to harvest shrimps from the tangab, a bamboo enclosure with net traps. I was awed by the tiny blue lights from within the shrimps which jumped about as the net was hoisted. We'd pick a few and drop them straight into our mouths.*
> — Fe A. Andico, in Journey (unpublished)

My aunt would build her interest in folklore and history into a career but, in the late 1960s, Aklan had no jobs for someone with her aspirations. She spent her early twenties caring for her dying father, watching her options eroded by each wave that crashed along the sea wall.

When she fell in love with an equally optionless local boy, her mother sent her further south to Mindanao to live with her older brother

When she fell in love with an equally optionless local boy, her mother sent her further south to Mindanao to live with her older brother. Among his students was a young physicist who would become her husband. They made their way across state universities until they secured professorships in Lingayen, capital of Pangasinan province in the North.

My aunt and I caught up with each other at university in the late 1980s. I was an undergraduate, she was completing her PhD. Her research explored the role of women in traditional fishing communities near Lingayen. 'Fishermen' was the wrong term, she told me, as I proofed her draft. And what was a 'fishwife'? What she had found was that couples shared the risks and labours of fishing, heading out to sea and spending moonless nights together on their boats. It was my introduction to the limitations of the language in which we learned and spoke about ourselves, and my first glimpse into the cavities of history where women had fallen.

I noted the pronounced changes in her demeanour each time I saw her. Her husband's alcohol-fuelled rages and infidelities had reduced her to a trembling globule of anxiety and helplessness. We all knew, we could see it happening. A steady, inexorable diminution that none of us could arrest. Every so often she sent me desperate text messages. She wanted to leave, she said, could she stay with me at my apartment?

Of course, I replied. After a few days of silence, she would ask me to find a lawyer or look up marriage statutes.

Leave now and we'll sort that later, I said, annoyed by her indecision.

I know you think I am weak, I'm not like your mother, she replied. This was our tense exchange in 2004, the year I came to England.

She stayed with her husband until his death eleven years later, her attempts at escape thwarted by fear or loyalty, maybe even love. She died alone at her home in Lingayen in 2019, two Octobers after she visited me in London. There were no warnings, no lingering illnesses to alarm us. She just went; the swift exit she was not able to make from her marriage.

Our mothers had prepared us for this life, we told ourselves, as we organised her funeral from across five countries. To move and adapt, to contain our grief. We decided to reclaim her one last time. She would never be reunited with her husband. We buried her next to her parents and mine.

———

The men treat their wives well and love them according to their habits and customs – although they are all barbarians and have no manners or politeness.

– Miguel Lopez de Legazpi,
in *Relation of the Filipinas Islands and of the character of their inhabitants* (undated)

The news of my aunt's death reached me on the same screen where I had been chatting with my cousins about her writings, uploaded in the weeks before her sudden passing. We were astonished by what she had uncovered. Our great-great maternal grandmother was a binukot by the name of Maria Masinda Dalida.

We have two dates for Maria's birth. The first, supplied by my aunt, is 1826. This would have made her 120 years old at her (recorded) death in 1946. Unlikely but possible. The other is 1865, a 'suggested' date from an online genealogy site. Whichever birth year is correct, it doesn't change the fact that her life traversed three colonial occupations. She spent her youth with her clan during the last century of Spanish rule, with her family in the lowlands of Aklan during the Philippine revolution and the early years of the American era, and her final years under the Japanese occupation. My mother's contemporaries still remember the ancient matriarch from their wartime childhoods, so revered that families vied to host her in their homes, to scent her hair with ylang-ylang oil and to listen to her stories.

My mother's contemporaries still remember the ancient matriarch from their wartime childhoods, so revered that families vied to host her in their homes

Maria was from Batan, south of Aklan. As her forename indicates, she was a Christian despite her Panay Bukidnon origins. Spanish missionaries had been in Panay for three centuries before her birth, almost everyone had been converted and renamed. Still, kinfolk called her by her mountain name, Ebe, whose meaning eludes us now.

My aunt reconstructs a clearer picture of Ebe's married years. She and her husband had six children, five sons and one daughter. He managed farmlands and a fishing fleet, she ran an enterprise making piña and abaca clothes. Years of isolation as a binukot had made her into an expert weaver and embroiderer, crafts she passed on to apprentices in a longhouse where she kept seven looms.

In an era where women were consigned to domesticity, Ebe had a livelihood and an independent income. She was literate and numerate despite the absence of any formal schooling. Had she possessed enough money to repay her dowry, she would have been free to divorce her husband according to customary law, although Catholic doctrine and Philippine state law forbade it (and still do). This is more than the lot of many Filipino women today.

How to feel, then, about a girl cloistered and pampered so she could keep her skin fair and her people's history alive, only to be married off to the highest bidder?

How to feel, then, about a girl cloistered and pampered so she could keep her skin fair and her people's history alive, only to be married off to the highest bidder? Each time I inspect the truths I think I've uncovered, I come away with layers of piña, a fabric braided from the fibre of pineapple leaves, more light than textile. She is somewhere underneath, swaddled in tissues of surrender and subterfuge.

—

That in a distant land I have a peer
In the person of a woman
A famed well-kept one
She's not from the Underworld
Nor from the Upperworld
But in a place where the sky
And sea meet, there she lives
– From verses 280-290 of *Epic of Central Panay 2,*
Hinilawod, Adventures of Humadapnon,
Chanted by Hugan-an, translated by F. Landa
Jocano (recorded in 1957, published in 2000)

Five hundred years ago this year, a local chieftain
called Lapu-lapu and his band of warriors killed
the Portuguese explorer Ferdinand Magellan in
Mactan, south-east of Panay, ending his ambition
to circumnavigate the world under the Spanish
flag. The next wave of Spanish administrators and
troops led by Miguel Lopez de Legazpi moved up
to the south of Panay in 1569. In the uplands they
came across more resisters with full-body tattoos,
strange legends suggesting a maritime past, women
with priestly status. This was the mythology that
Jocano stumbled upon in 1955.

Apart from being storytellers, binukot like
Hugan-an and Ebe were themselves characters in
these epic tales. The Hinilawod features binukot
protagonists such as Matan-ayon who, trapped in a
marriage to a dishonourable husband, transforms
herself into water every night. He must collect every
drop if he wants to see her whole again.

She and her daughter, Nagmalitong Yawâ, turn themselves into male warriors to rescue datus-in-distress such as the noble Humadapnon, trapped in an island cave by legions of enchantresses (also binukot). He is liberated by Nagmalitong Yawâ, who disguises herself as a man to spare his pride. Upon being freed, he sets off again on another adventure, returns after seven years to find his rescuer betrothed to another man. He kills her and the wedding party.

In the tales, binukot are high-born mortals, mothers and wives of rulers, arbiters of disputes, conduits among the earthly, the divine and all beings inhabiting the layers in between. This is mirrored in the practical realm, where the binukot's mastery of the clan's history and arts was only made possible by a social hierarchy and a system of servitude. It took significant resources for subsistence communities to spare members from agricultural or domestic work: a retinue of mentors to educate her, servants to bathe her in the river at night, brothers and attendants to carry her around in a covered hammock so her feet never touch the ground.

In this narrative tradition, a binukot is not a passive chronicler, she is embedded within the stories. She honours the names of places, gods and ancestors, the few solid elements she has inherited. She adjudicates. Which god's vanity is mocked, which injustice preserved for future judgement? What strategies must she employ to stay alive in body and memory?

Imagine generations of storytellers trained to remember that valour and wisdom had always been the province of women. This was my aunt's parting gift and I am now its custodian.

I was still in primary school, and possibly Ate Ofelia was in high school, when I suffered from excessive coughing. Mother said that the sea breeze was a possible remedy and tasked Ate to take me daily to Manila Bay. Ate and I would stay on the sea wall for some time, breathing, filling in my lungs with the salty, balmy morning breeze until the sun rose and its heat warmed our skin.
— Fe A. Andico in *Journey* (unpublished)

I've found another October shared with my aunt. It is from 1975. A procession of hurricanes arrives that month like devotees in nimbus veils. I am imprisoned at home by the rains with my sister and my brother. My aunt has travelled to Manila to give birth to a fragile boy, and they are staying with us in our crumbling house.

One afternoon my mother cradles the baby when the wind flings a window onto her back. I remember the moment of contact, the clatter and the screaming and, in the aftermath, a purple continent of bruises on my mother's skin. My aunt, in a written account of that afternoon, remembers the slab as a disused bed frame resting against the bedroom wall. But if it was against the wall, how did the wind slam it onto my mother's body with such violence?

She takes the blow, shielding my cousin's weeks-old skull. My aunt weeps with relief. She had lost her first child years before, a daughter starved of oxygen in a far-flung town. My mother soothes her. They sit together in that room for days and days, their faces illumined by lightning, surrounded by squealing children thrilled by the spectacle of a restless infant and sky. **H**

Abebe

the cook's son

by Chris Beckett

He is tall and slim, with thick short hair, an open shirt, skinny jeans and sky-blue trainers. He stands there looking you full in the face and there is not an ounce of fat on his body or of shyness in his gaze. He is sixteen, to my eight, and as far as I'm concerned, he is a god. I would love to rest a hand on my hip, like Abebe. I would love to be Abebe's hip and have his hand rest on me like on a horse's neck.

When is the moment that I first become aware of him? There is a process you might know, called imprinting, whereby young creatures become attached to the first living object they encounter. The shell cracks and a wet beaky head appears, looking his mother in the eye. Anyone the poult sees in this moment is his mother. He will look up bleary-eyed, and if it's you, he'll press his face against your cheek and fall asleep.

That's how it is the first time I see Abebe. I am a born boy, but born again when I see Abebe. My shell breaks, my little slouch stands straight, my freckles bounce all over my face, when I see Abebe. And how do I know this? Well, I remember it, I think – not when and where exactly, but how it feels, the way my eyes get stuck on him, the shocking sleepiness of it. And look! my shoulders droop in photos when he is not there. He sparks a light in me, unties the little knot of queerness in my chest. From then on, somewhere deep within my chromosomes, I start to watch him, follow him, love him.

I only know Abebe for about three years, in the mid-1960s, while my family lives in Addis Ababa, before my dad is posted like a letter back to London. In that time I never touch Abebe, nor he me. We speak, I hear his voice. We spend a lot of time together and his presence puts a frame around the minutes, hours, afternoons. Only three years, but when I turn around, he's always here, right next to me, the first line of a poem…

Abebe, from a distant afternoon…

Sometimes, if I'm lucky, a poem hits the page running, sure of itself, cocky almost. *Abebe, the cook's son* is one of these jobby poems that make me smile as I write. It sprints along the path in front of me, looking back occasionally over its shoulder with a pitying glance, as if it thinks I'm pretty stupid not to have guessed where it is going. Still, I don't mind, just happy to be led.

But it has actually been a long time coming: my first poem about Ethiopia happens when I am fourteen, at school in England, immersed in D.H. Lawrence's exciting animal poems, like *Humming Bird* and *Fish*. His *Snake* reminds me of a camping trip to Lake Langano, one of the Great Rift Valley lakes. We are driving back to Addis in our creamy Ford Zephyr, singing 'Tipperary' or 'Waltzing Matilda', as Dad swerves round potholes and fish eagles squabble in the acacia trees. Plastic seat covers leech to our under thighs. Now we stop to stretch our legs and air the car of dust. Only after getting out and loafing around, do we realise that we are next to a crocodile swamp, and a herder is coming towards us with a twelve-foot rock python wired at the throat.

'I felt so honoured,' says Lawrence when his snake appears. And so do I, in a shivery way. Pythons are slow, they lie in wait, but when they strike, they wrap you in their coils and crush you dead in a minute! Antelope, kudu, goats, even a crocodile. Boys, too, yes. Sergeant Abbe who takes me riding has told me about the dozy unsuspecting boys out there in the bush or by a lake who end up in a python's belly. But this snake hangs from the man's hand, flaps about like a fish on the grass. We stand there dazed, my mum and dad, my sisters, gripped by the knife that slits his green-gold body open, by the tube of gore sliced out of him before our eyes. His spitting little head comes off so quickly too and now his skin is wrapped in paper and sulking on the back window of the car, not far from my right ear.

I love the way Lawrence describes his snake, how simply he presents the facts, with courtesy and wonder. It doesn't feel strange to read 'and truly I was afraid' or 'thrice adream', to hear the repetitions 'must wait, must stand and wait…' So I slip into a boy-Lawrence voice to write my poem. But unlike Lawrence, I sound ponderous. I hate my vague othering words like 'African' and 'rags' to describe the herder. I do not have the confidence to call him simply 'Ethiopian', so I generalise and in the process distance my reader, and myself too, from the story of the poem. Nor do I wonder how an Ethiopian poet might see my snake or write about it, what his or her snake praises might sound like. Perhaps you are furthest away from something, when you don't even notice the distance.

Her teeth shine like Haile Selassie's palace at night, thanks to a pocket trove of toothpick twigs

Over the years, I travel further into a style that tries to force my boyhood into poetic forms that have nothing to do with Ethiopia. Perhaps the farthest I go is a sonnet about our lovely *gered* (maid) Aster, a shy young woman with a soft laugh. She lives in a skinny lean-to against the back wall and is fanatical about dusting. Her teeth shine like Haile Selassie's palace at night, thanks to a pocket trove of toothpick twigs. She also has a *gered* of her own, even younger and more giggly, who braids Aster's hair on her afternoons off. There is a motherly gentleness about Aster, slightly aloof but in a kind way, that makes me think of the Virgin Mary – and, sure enough, when my parents buy a traditional Ethiopian pietà on parchment, I think it looks exactly like Aster. You do not have to read my sonnet to imagine its regular iambs, its discreet rhymes, how it plays with likenesses. At one point Aster jumps into the painting and I see the Virgin Mary frowning at a spot of dust…

My subject is Ethiopia but my form is Shakespeare. In one way this is OK: Aster works for an English household, so she inhabits an English 'poem house', a sonnet. But what do sonnets have to do with Aster or Ethiopia? Isn't it a sort of cultural imperialism, I ask myself, to write about Africa in an English literary form; what Malawian poet Felix Mnthali angrily called the 'stranglehold of English lit' in his poem of the same name?

English lit, my sister,
was more than a cruel joke –
it was the heart
of alien conquest.

Aimé Césaire dances his jailbreak dance, a breaking-the-yoke dance. Wole Soyinka insists that Africans must inhabit their own centre, tap their own artistic traditions, write their own richly detailed contexts. The little white boy in Addis Ababa may be neither one thing nor t'other, no Ethiopian roots of his own to dig up, but he knows one thing: that Ethiopian soldiers thrashed the Italians at Adwa in 1896, and that Haile Selassie is boss here, not a white governor. This is where the African Union is based, where African flags deck the avenues on Inauguration Day in 1963. And look, here's Dad coming home from the opening ceremony, jumping out of his car and shouting

Africa United!!

My parents' friends are Ato Endelkachew and his wife, Weizero Wubit. My love is called Abebe, not Stephen or Mark. I am not thinking about cultural or literary theory, nor the politics of 1960s Ethiopia. I just want my poems to rub skin with their subjects, to summon them from a place and time quite far away. Or perhaps it is truer to say that I want to summon myself to them, fly over seas and deserts, over the mountains of Gheralta pocked with rock churches, over the Blue Nile surging past hillsides of t'eff. I want to get out of what feels like the departure lounge of my writing, finally board the plane.

So I start looking for Ethiopian poems to set my head on fire, to teach me new rhythms, phrases, ways of seeing and saying things that resonate with my childhood. A boy may not speak Amharic fluently but his ears have memories. So I take language classes at the School of Oriental and African Studies (SOAS) in London. Then with my friend Alemu, we start translating the short punchy verses of a young poet I've met in Addis called Bewketu Seyoum. We also march up the foothills of an extraordinary long poem – *Berekete Mergem/ The Gift of a Curse* – by exiled poet Gemoraw, one of Alemu's heroes. The poem lambasts scientists around the world for inventing things which are then used to control and abuse people. It is a diatribe against progress and Gemoraw shouts it at a university event in front of Haile Selassie, who is so disgusted that he storms out. Meanwhile, I spend hours in the SOAS library, leafing through old copies of the *Journal of the Institute of Ethiopian Studies*, hunting poems from all areas and languages of Ethiopia. What I find (or what finds me?) are Praise Poems for people and animals, Warrior Boasts, Ironic Boasts (in the voices of disease or hunger), anti-corruption Wails, Insults, Student Protests like Mohammed Idris' *Dusk to Dawn*, in which his rickety old bed stands for Ethiopia, full of vicious blood-sucking bugs.

These poems spring out of their pages like hyenas with a barking, jack-in-the box quality of surprise

These poems spring out of their pages like hyenas with a barking, jack-in-the box quality of surprise. I enjoy every second of reading them and even though Abebe is not a shouty boy, I catch his light glottal voice ringing in my ear, brandishing these lists with their syntactical repetitions like 'you, who…' or 'the one who…', or 'O Nasero, my magnificent ox…!' When you hear an Ethiopian praise poem, I realise, you become the object of its praise, the 'you, who' is being addressed, even the farmer's 'magnificent ox'. Similarly, if you write a praise poem, then maybe whoever reads or listens to it becomes the person, the ox, this endlessly inclusive 'you'?

Gradually, surrounded by the mutter of these shelves, the restless crowds of Ethiopian books, I begin to imagine myself as a small praise-singing boy, stood a little awkwardly perhaps on the third step of a big white-painted house in Addis Ababa, its garden packed with mesqal daisies, dogs and horses, donkeys, maids, cooks, houseboys, parents, sisters, priests, old ladies, passers-by. And then a beautiful Ethiopian prince appears out of the kitchen door, strides into the small circle of tarmac by the gates, plants his feet apart and faces me. There is not an ounce of fat on his body, no shyness in his gaze. His shirt is open-necked, his sky-blue trainers spotless. He smiles and, right now, in the SOAS library off Russell Square, from somewhere deep within myself, I start to sing Abebe's praise. **H**

Abebe, the cook's son

Abebe, from a distant afternoon
Abebe, from an afternoon where everybody naps
even the donkeys propped against trees
    on their little hoofs
Abebe, tall as a eucalyptus tree
Abebe, black all over when he pisses on a
    eucalyptus tree
who jaunties down dirt tracks to the honey shop
    buys two drippy honeycombs in a box
Abebe, the cool boy in drain-pipe jeans and sky-
    blue sneakers
Abebe, the busy crossing where girls stop to chat
who clicks his fingers to the funky Ibex Band
    as we saunter back up track
Abebe, calling *come here!* to the dog called Come Here
Abebe, trotting round the dog-yard like a horse
who saddles up the smoky horses and takes me
    prairie-galloping
who makes a dash at mud-caves where hyenas sleep
who shows me how to cook *kwalima* beef and ginger
    sausages
    and a chick-pea fish for Lent
Abebe, gobbling up the afternoon like a *kwalima*
Abebe, grinning like a chick-pea fish
    while everybody naps

In

of

Search

Lost Voices

by Jon Paul Roberts

1

A fox, sleek with an autumn colour and ears pushed back, froze when it saw me. It waited, assessing my threat level, and then appeared to soften. I opened my mouth to speak, to say hello delicately like I might to a dog or cat, but the word caught in my throat. It was as if my unlubricated gullet held it hostage, and when it did finally emerge, it spluttered out like it didn't have enough support from my own body. To the fox, this was startling and it slinked away into the street without looking back.

This happened when I lived in London, aged twenty-three, and my housemate was away on a research trip. Sitting on the front step of our building in NW, around 11pm, trying to speak to a fox, I realised that I hadn't spoken to anyone in the past twenty-four hours. I hadn't spoken on the phone, hadn't been to any shop where the basic 'do you need a carrier bag' conversation might happen with a cashier, hadn't even spoken to myself around the house. Instead, I'd trundled from bed to sofa to stoop, in silence, laptop in hand trying to write and, when I became distracted, endlessly scrolling through job adverts online.

The following day, simply to speak, I called my grandma, who then aged eighty-nine, didn't often talk much on the phone, or at all, yet she regularly chastised me for not calling enough. Sometimes, I imagined our conversations as they might appear in a movie by Chantal Akerman, still shots of the lonely city I was living in passing by whilst superficial trivialities passed between us. She preferred to listen: university was fine, there was a lot of reading (most of which I wasn't doing); I had left my job at a charity that had mostly involved me standing in the cold entryways of churches or community centres across the city selling Christmas cards, so I was looking for whatever work I could find; and, yes, I was eating enough (though I most definitely wasn't.)

What else have you been doing? she asked, even though I'd exhausted every other topic. She said, I just like hearing your voice.

I started rambling about the minutia of life in the city, nothing too specific. I could not discuss with her the writers I was reading at the time: Michelle Tea, Édouard Louis, or Alison Bechdel. Firstly, because I had never seen her read anything other than the TV guide or the tabloid news, so a conversation about books would consist of me explaining what happened within them. Secondly, the idea, then, of describing radical lesbian poetry nights or early explorations of sexuality felt off-limits, as if it might reveal something about myself that wasn't known to her. Instead, I offered idle talk about Tube lines, the fact that everything was so connected, the places I avoided. She occasionally umm'd and ahh'd, but provided nothing substantial in the way of a response.

Desperately not wanting to hear my voice much longer, I hassled her for some information about her life, of which she was never overly forthcoming. Not too bad, she said. She had done the usual: been shopping, picked up her pension from the Post Office – which she always took out in cash – and let the dog in and out of the garden. His Lordship, she said, had a way of telling her when he wanted to be let out, pawing and nudging her at regular intervals throughout the day, and she was no longer sure who was in charge. When she finished, there was silence.

She used her voice sparingly, especially in later years. It was as if her proximity to death had taken something from her too

Silence often punctuated our phone calls. I called her partly out of obligation because, at the time, very little was happening in my life to report in earnest. My dad, her son, had been dead for nearly five years; her husband, my grandad, almost ten. Outside of our phone calls and her occasional trips to the supermarket or hairdressers, she spent a lot of her time alone. She used her voice sparingly, especially in later years. It was as if her proximity to death had taken something from her too. She took time to recall people's names or the item in the kitchen she wanted you to get, and her insecurity around the disappearance of words left her rattled. She would simply not answer a question if she didn't understand it. Whether it came from a doctor or me, she would sit in silence. It was as if not acknowledging it meant it didn't exist.

When I returned home in a few weeks, I knew I would be met with indignance because I hadn't called enough. That she would speak in a pointed tone, saying things like, So you do exist! In those stretched-out days when she rose at 5am and went to bed at 7pm, she had time to think about my absence and failures. I regularly wondered what other thoughts filled her head during those long hours. Did she fantasise, as I did on the Tube, of outlandish romantic scenarios or what alternative paths life could take? Did she run over conversations she'd had, editing herself to arrive at the best outcome? Did she try to re-create those voices that were now gone; of her son? Her husband? Did she hear them? Did they speak to her? I knew, if I asked, she would never tell.

As I write this, five years after the phone conversation, I try to think of my grandma's voice, to describe how it might sound. She has been dead for two years, and her voice slipped away almost instantly. I can't hear the sounds she used to make, the Liverpool accent she never lost, or her exact pitch, timbre and tone as she tried to convince me to stay home instead of going out. I can only remember how her voice made me feel: warm, safe, sometimes irritated. I can just imagine this in the abstract, of course. To feel like this again exactly, I would need her voice. What is it about the human voice that causes it to disappear so quickly? And would I ever hear her voice again?

After we hung up that day, I typed: 'can we remember the voices of the dead' into the search bar of my phone. A result from Quora, a question-and-answer site, popped up with a query about whether it is 'normal' to forget your mother's voice. It was posted on December 6th 2015, and the answer was surprisingly short: yes, it's absolutely normal.

...I grab for it, only to find it slipping even further away. How much would I give to hear her voice again?

Now, when I type those words into my search bar, I find a journalist, Laura Kennedy, has written in the *Irish Times* about her mother's voice: 'When I try to recall it, as I am now, something in me reaches out and waits, quietly, as though expecting her to call up the stairs to me the way she used to do. Everything is still, but the voice doesn't come. I haven't heard it in three years, and I will never hear it again.'

2

I wasn't a kid who asked for stories before bed, but my grandma would occasionally sing songs to me. They weren't nursery rhymes, but often lullabies she'd heard growing up or songs my granddad sang at the local working men's club, usually Frank Sinatra or Bing Crosby-esque standards.

We played one of these songs at her funeral, Crosby's deep masculine voice replacing her softer one. The song was called 'Too-Ra-Loo-Ra-Loo-Ral (That's an Irish Lullaby)' and was written in 1913 by the Irish-American composer James Royce Shannon. We chose it because she used to sing it to us, but of course, as children we had no idea what the song was about. Instead, it was about her voice which, when singing, was weak and heady but soft. Looking at the lyrics now, it takes on a new kind of relevance:

> *Over in Killarney, many years ago*
> *My mither sang a song to me in tones so sweet and low,*
> *Just a simple little ditty, in her good ould Irish way,*
> *And I'd give the world if she could sing*
> *That song to me this day.*

The image I get now, of someone separated from their mother by a great distance, aching to hear their voice again, sits within me. So I try to think of her voice singing the song, but it floats hazily in my mind. Every time I think it's appearing, I grab for it, only to find it slipping even further away. How much would I give to hear her voice again? My grandma's voice, like that of my dad's and grandad's, is gone. I do not hear it every day or, more accurately, I cannot hear it.

When I talk about this with a friend one night, she says it's the opposite for her. 'I can remember sounds really well', she says, 'but it's faces I can't imagine.'

For me, I have the faces in my mind, though I question the value of them. They are nothing that can't be found in photos. But sound, the voice in motion, feels so different.

'Do they make you feel any better', I ask. 'Do you find them reassuring?'

She isn't sure. She hasn't thought about whether the sentences she can hear in her head are real or if they're made up. But she has, stored in her brain, what I want. She can re-create, envision, and imagine sounds. I feel, during this conversation, a fit of immense jealousy.

3

Sound conjures images as clear as day; it throws a hook into the depths of memory and punctures specific pieces, pulling the almost-forgotten to the surface like elusive silverfish that swim along the bed. Anytime I hear 'Stay' by Shakespeare's Sister, I immediately see the winding Scottish road I first heard it on while driving with my family on a trip in my teen years. Or catching the certain rhythm of a landline ringtone, I'm suddenly stood by the chunky plastic house phone of my youth, waiting for my friend to call me back. What I hadn't considered before was that sound itself did not seem conjurable to me. Instead, these sounds came whilst I was writing in cafés or stood in the queue at the supermarket. What's more, the places to which they take me back didn't seem accessible in any other way. I wondered then, where my grandma's voice might transport me. I did not need to remember her image. I could see that clearly: permed brunette hair, glasses, a supermarket-bought button-up sundress, her near-perfect smile aided by dentures she soaked in a glass each night with a tablet that fizzed like an experiment. But I did not find these images reassuring; an image doesn't feel like it can reassure. It feels far, disconnected, unresponsive. I wanted to see where her voice would take me in my memory, what certain phrases would summon from that inaccessible part of my mind. Still, it felt like a strange fixation; of all the things I'd lost when she died, her voice was seemingly my primary focus, and it all felt impossible until I started to research it.

I wanted to see where her voice would take me in my memory, what certain phrases would summon from that inaccessible part of my mind

I came across a Yale University study that found our sense of hearing is even more accurate than our sense of sight in identifying emotions. In a way, this explained my fixation; it was about her emotional essence. When we can only hear a person's voice – rather than see their facial expressions along with it – our attention is drawn to its specific subtleties, meaning it might be easier to glean someone's emotional state over the phone. A scientist in London has used a 3D printer to re-create a specific person's vocal tract: Nesyamun, an Egyptian priest who died some 3,000 years ago. Then, I came across a clip from a BBC show called *Neanderthal: The Rebirth* featuring vocal coach Patsy Rodenburg and, I assume, a student of hers. I sat at my desk, playing the clip over and over. Rodenburg suggested what Neanderthal vocalisations might have sounded like – high-pitched screeches rather than the low grunts we previously believed they used. She assessed that this was likely due to their body shape and size as well as a vocal tract that differed from ours. These scientists and specialists understood the complexities of the voice.

However, there was a study at Cornell University that used artificial intelligence-based voice cloning software to re-create voices from five-second clips. After learning the 'essence of human speech' in only five seconds, the software could infer the sounds it didn't hear and re-create the voice near perfectly. The re-created voice clips sounded spookily similar to the original clip, except for a very slight digitised edge to them.

This is all I would need: a VCR recording of a birthday party, an answering machine message, voice notes recorded on tape

I thought of my friends, whose parents existed in my childhood memories with video cameras taped to their hands. I thought of how those friends had the sounds they wanted. They would have more than five seconds, should they wish to follow this crazed line of thinking too. But my grandma was careful to avoid video cameras, and we as a family couldn't afford our own. That is all I would need; a VCR recording of a birthday party, an answering machine message, voice notes recorded on tape.

If I could track down five seconds of my grandma's voice, I could hear it again, saying anything I might ask it to. I might have it say 'Not too bad'; a phrase she used that I have now adopted, one that pessimistically framed her mood in relation to the bad, the negative, which is implied as the normal state. I might ask it to say the things she told others about herself, about me. My family would impress upon me how proud my grandma had been of my choices – she kept a framed copy of my degree certificate in her living room and often told others I was doing great things in the City – but she never vocalised any of this to me. When we were together, she would speak, as I did, of mundanities. Maybe, if I could re-create her voice, I could ask it to say the words she reserved for others. Of course, without any trace of her voice, this is impossible.

4

In the autumn of 2017, about nine months after the fox and the phone call, I moved back to my hometown to live with my grandma. London had wrung me dry, financially and emotionally, so I was looking to reset. Between September and December, our relationship returned to how it had been. At times, I felt infantilised, and we bickered about my staying out too late or the shows I watched on TV. But we rarely *talked*. Now that we could just be in each other's presence, staring blankly at a screen or manoeuvring in the kitchen as I cooked us dinner, we didn't feel the need to fill it with words. It was a comfortable silence. Not one I felt disturbed by or was overly aware of. It wasn't like being on the phone when silence is amplified; it felt like a strangely relaxed symbiosis.

On Christmas Eve that year, she had a stroke, a minor one, and, as an X-Ray showed, it was not her first. This led to a year of rapid deterioration in which she stopped speaking and could no longer ask for anything, even if she wanted to. She went in and out of the hospital, and when she was home, she required carers to visit her six times a day – all of this to avoid a care home; somewhere she had always said she never wanted to go.

What I noticed most during her illness were the ways in which she was bypassed. Seeing her age and diagnosis, a doctor would speak directly to me – even in her presence. I couldn't tell if this was due to my perceived maleness or youth, but they would ask personal questions – when she had last been to the toilet, how her bowel movements had been, what her mood was like – and I, the supposed conduit, would answer for her. I regret now that I didn't push back on that dehumanising approach to her care, which removed any sense of autonomy, but I understood it. I had felt myself becoming irritated when she couldn't answer simple questions, when she refused to offer anything in response. I knew it wasn't her fault, and I was ashamed each time I noticed it in myself, but it was there. The silence that followed a question sometimes grew so long I wanted to scream. I would try to rephrase the question, but it somehow would become more muddled until, eventually, I gave up. In that sense, I was complicit in her silencing and oversaw the loss of her voice like a foreman, mindlessly aware of how it was all progressing.

What did it mean for her to be voiceless? Silenced? In myth, it was a punishment; the nymph Echo condemned only to repeat what she heard, never able to offer anything new. In Homer's

Odyssey, Penelope was silenced by her son for disagreeing. Hans Christian Anderson's mermaid gave up speech as the price of love, foolishly, as the price for hope. In a modern sense, it feels explicitly political. In a 2017 essay for *The Guardian*, Rebecca Solnit wrote: 'If our voices are essential aspects of our humanity, to be rendered voiceless is to be dehumanised or excluded from one's humanity.' These historical and fictional examples consider a lack of voice as both a punishment and a personal failure. We may desire quietness, a space to think, ruminate, and find peace, but if we are silenced, we are forced into not talking, despite having something to say.

I have often wondered, if my grandma were in a myth or a fairy-tale, what might be considered her transgression?

I have often wondered, if my grandma were in a myth or a fairy-tale, what might be considered her transgression? In reality, her punishment was not spun as part of a story. She was simply growing old, reminding those who saw her that life was finite.

5

In the time I spent on hospital wards, I noticed how often older women were denied their voice. In these often-gendered spaces, I saw women being talked over and ignored.

Once, when I was visiting my grandma with my aunt, during one of her lengthy hospital stays, a woman in a private room just across from my grandma's bed was screaming out for help. If my grandma noticed the commotion, she didn't show it. Nurses passed the room, and occasionally one might stick their head in and tell the woman to calm down. God help me, the woman kept screaming. God, please help me. Nurses looked at us with apologetic faces; what could be done?

We sat, trying to form a conversation while the screaming rattled us. It went on for what felt like hours but was, in reality, about thirty minutes before my aunt stood and poked her head around the door and asked: I'm not God, but what can I do?

...my aunt stood and poked her head around the door and asked: I'm not God, but what can I do?

For a while, my aunt sat with the woman, offered to make her comfortable, and listened to her talk – which the nurses assured us were nonsense ramblings. Listening, as it was then, as it is now, is often the answer to voicelessness. To be voiceless, in the metaphorical sense, is not to be heard. Yet, as much as I wanted to listen, something within me – guilt? Panic? Fear? – didn't do enough.

I noticed this denial in other family members, too, not just staff. How, often, they would discount what their loved one said and how they would hold forth during visits, speaking at length about the trivialities of their existence outside the hospital. I recognised in this a sense of self-protection, a refusal to fully accept how their older relative had been impacted. Much is said of denial after death but rarely do we discuss it in anticipation of death.

As the weeks went on, and I realised my grandma's voice was fading along with every other part of herself. I realised I could do little to save it, and I was also aware that I had lost my voice around my grandma too. Culturally, there was a divide between us, and I found that I lacked the words to talk about my life with her. Even before her illness, there had been no way to broach my queer life, which was, admittedly, in turmoil. I had been dating a man for the first time in years, but I wasn't able to tell him that my grandma was sick. Instead, I grew distant and found things about him to pick at: he smoked too much weed, he didn't ask enough questions. I couldn't tell this to her, nor could I tell her about the men I slept with after we broke up. I couldn't discuss the radical drag nights I was going to, the discussions I was having, the books I was reading, the complex and ongoing confusion around my gender identity, because I hadn't found the words to tell her I was queer at all.

Years before, she had raised her shoulders in discomfort, said it wasn't right that two men were kissing on some late-night television drama. For years, she had called my female friends my 'girlfriends' to other family members, no matter how many times I corrected her. For years, I used these as reasons to curtail a conversation. If she didn't have long left, I told myself, why would I risk ruining our relationship even if it meant that relationship was filled with holes. This was also a type of silencing; never allowing her to grow or face my queerness. And so I spoke for her, decided that was enough to make my decision.

When I look back on the period that she was sick, I realise we both needed to be cared for. She found that in me, in the nurses and doctors. I found it with men online, in hotel rooms, in bedrooms in the middle of the day. She was scared of dying, I was scared of her dying. We couldn't talk about that, so we did not talk. Or, rather, I didn't try hard enough to talk to her. I let her slip into silence, and then I, like Orpheus into hell, followed her.

6

A friend of mine works for a charity that assigns advocates to work with elderly clients who don't have family members to fight for them. Her job is to assess a client's best interest, whether that is staying at home, seeking out care or considering the financial implications. As a voice for those who need it, her role is how I tried to reconfigure my position in my grandma's life, but I was never able to fully make that leap. I spoke for her, made decisions, and tried to evaluate all of the information to make the best ones. Yet, years later, I still feel guilt and something like regret.

In August 2018, my grandma moved into a care home around the corner from where we lived. Something she had never wanted to do. When I brought it up to her, said that at-home care was costing nearly £1500 a month and the care company was suggesting she needed more – she required round-the-clock care and couldn't be left alone – she didn't protest. She simply nodded and turned to look out the window.

Once she moved, I'm not entirely sure she knew where she was, if she didn't think she was back on another hospital ward. She lay in bed or occasionally sat in her chair – put there by one of the nurses – and stared into space. She refused, more times than not, to join the other residents in communal areas, and any time I visited, she was in her room. I bought a radio and placed it on her dresser, but she paid little attention to whether it was on or not. She rarely spoke. In fact, I can't recall a single word she said to me after she moved in. She would nod, indicate whether she wanted you to do what you'd just suggested or not, but never said so.

She lay in bed or occasionally sat in her chair – put there by one of the nurses – and stared into space

For the past two years I have considered why, living at home, she declined slowly, but once she moved, it was rapid. From December to February, there had been talk of recovery. From February to August, discussion of 'final stages', until September when she died after just a month in the home.

I had gone against her wishes – ones she had made clear in her younger days – and maybe that was the final act. Her voice was finally gone, faded until it could be ignored or overruled. I knew that living at home was no longer possible. It was dangerous, costly, and didn't provide all she needed, but that didn't mean I felt vindicated.

I thought then of my voice on the porch, all those years earlier. About how, after only twenty-four hours on my own, it had lost its ability to arrive seamlessly, without splutter. Over the final year of her life, my grandma's voice crept back inside of her and did not often come out. So much so that, as I sat with her by her deathbed, I could not remember her voice; even then, I could not hear it. I could only hear the strange, uneven breathing of someone who is about to stop. In the years since, I have searched for her voice, have tried to reinstate it out of guilt, out of grief.

In one of his poems, Thomas Hardy imagines that he can hear the voice of a woman calling out to him. 'The Voice', first published in 1914, is often said to be about his wife, Emma Gifford, who died in 1912 after twenty-eight years of marriage. 'Woman much missed, how you call to me,' he wrote. 'Can it be you that I hear? Let me view you, then […] Or is it only the breeze in its listlessness […] You being ever dissolved to wan witlessness / Heard no more again far or near?'

I'm afraid, for the rest of my life, it will always be the listless breeze. ▪

The Real Story

D E V E L O P I N G C R E A T I V E N O N F I C T I O N
A N D T H E E S S A Y I N T H E U K

The Real Story is a Manchester-based writer development project and online journal devoted to promoting the form of creative nonfiction writing in the UK. Funded by Arts Council England, we provide workshops, mentoring and a publishing platform for both established and emerging creative nonfiction talent. We're always looking for personal essays and pitches, so head over to therealstory.org/submit and send us something wonderful.

Supported using public funding by

ARTS COUNCIL ENGLAND

IN CONVERSATION WITH
Doireann Ní Ghríofa

Poet and essayist Doireann Ní Ghríofa won the James Tait Black Prize for Biography for her book A Ghost in the Throat, *which was also named the Irish Book Awards Book of the Year 2020. Her first work of prose, it has been described as a genre-defying work of hybridity. Hinterland co-editor Yin F. Lim sat down with Doireann recently for a conversation about writing lives – our own and that of others – and playing with form when doing so, exploring the merging of non-fiction and fiction, and reclaiming the voices of women erased from historical records.*

Yin F. Lim: How did your book come about, and how long did it take to write?

Doireann Ní Ghríofa: *A Ghost in the Throat* is very much the story of a quest that occurred in reality in my life, and then took a slightly different form within the book. And whenever anyone asks me how long it took to write the book, I always say: the baby whose birth is described in the book is now six years old.

Now when I think about it, it all feels like a blur because it was such a journey of obsession, but I felt I was almost being drawn along by it. Some books can be like that. Other books are very clear in the point at which the writing process begins, and the point at which it ends. But this one certainly veered much more towards malleability; it's difficult to pinpoint its beginnings.

YFL: So the book came about from the quest?

DNG: Yeah, because so much of the book is concerned with speaking the story of another woman who lived centuries before I did: Eibhlín Dubh Ní Chonaill, the poet who composed the extraordinary poem *Caoineadh Airt Uí Laoghaire*. So much of the work I was trying to do required gathering biographical details about her life and trying to get a sense of the texture of her days and what it might have felt like to be her, to live in a very different Ireland as it was at the time.

I was almost performing research for this book, chasing details of her life long before I realised I was writing a book, because it was a very genuine curiosity to begin with, which became an obsessive interest in this other woman's life. So that's an interesting way to embark on a project!

YFL: In its back-cover blurb, *A Ghost in the Throat* is described as both essay and auto-fiction. Why call it auto-fiction as opposed to memoir?

DNG: As I was writing the book, it became clear to me that although most of the book drew very much on my own lived reality, and on the factual elements I could find on Eibhlín Dubh Ní Chonaill's life, there were also moments where the writing veered away into imagining, and into a more fictional understanding of certain moments. I wanted to follow that urgency, to have a mixture of form: biography, autobiography, but also to complicate it with a sense of imagining and fiction as well. Once I started to allow the fog of fiction into the book, there were so many other genres of writing that I wanted to welcome in as well, like a whole chapter on the literary translation of a poem. In retrospect, I'm glad that I took those chances.

But it's important, I think, for anyone who's interested in exploring the merging of non-fiction and fiction, to alert the reader to our methods. We trust our readers and our readers trust us. So it was very important for me to be really open with the reader and to flag very clearly to them that while this book is in many respects biography, it also has fictional elements. In hindsight, I'm not sure if auto-fiction is an accurate description, but I do feel that label does its work in alerting readers to the fact that this is not a purely factual biography...that the book you're about to read is a strange book. Get ready.

YFL: It felt like the more you got to know Eibhlín Dubh's story, the more you almost wanted to inhabit her life. There are parts of it that are just beautifully reimagined.

DNG: I suppose it's a kind of insatiability, the fact that no matter how much information I was seeking out, no matter how many new insights I was finding, it never felt like enough. Every new piece of information felt as though I was taking a step closer to Eibhlín Dubh Ní Chonaill's life. And yet I could never feel as close as I wanted to.

YFL: So you filled these gaps in her story through what you call a 'mishmash of daydream and fact.' At what point did you move from archival research into this reimagining of her life?

DNG: I think those two processes occur in parallel. In the Irish language we have a phrase – 'fite fuaite' – to describe how two quite disparate threads may be woven together, or intertwined. I had that feeling throughout this journey, in trying to investigate a life and the ethical questions that arise, the frustrations of how an author might go about imagining their way into the silences where the historical records fail us. They were all questions that I found very interesting. *A Ghost in the Throat* is not simply a chronological biography of Eibhlín Dubh Ní Chonaill's life, it's also an attempt to implicate the reader in the discovery of her life. I wanted the reader to join me in a kind of shared wandering through the more difficult elements of finding her story, through the mysteries of her life and the questions to which we will probably never have answers.

YFL: Yet you also question if you have the right to reimagine her life; what you call 'stitching frills on patterns.' You mention in the book that you felt like you were trespassing, that this re-creation of Eibhlín Dubh's life seemed like a form of thievery.

DNG: I find it interesting to consider biography in terms of thieving the facts of another person's life and repurposing them in a narrative. I very often wondered, if my subject were alive, whether she would slap me in the face and say: 'how dare you assume that you have the right to create a narrative of my life? How dare you?'

I imagine that many biographical subjects might feel the same way. And I feel that, for any of us who feel an urge towards writing biography, it's imperative that we turn such questions on ourselves as well: how would I feel if after my death, someone came along and rooted through my underwear drawer? Imagine someone finding all the scattered facts of our lives, and putting them together in the way that they perceive it. Imagine not having any control over how someone else will tell your story. So I felt that it was important to allow the reader into those questions that were coming up for me about what right I had to attempt to write a story of someone else's life.

YFL: You also put a lot of yourself in this story of your quest for Eibhlín Dubh Ní Chonaill's life.

DNG: There's a biography that I love, of Máire Rua, a really fierce woman who centuries ago lived in the area of Clare in the West of Ireland near where I grew up. It was written in the 1980s by a celebrated scholar called Máire MacNéill and published posthumously. It's a spectacular work of Máire Rua's life; I am in awe at the amount of scholarship and research that MacNéill had done. But I also wanted to know more about her attempts, and the frustrations she must have faced to find these details of Máire Rua's life, and there was none of that aspect of the research revealed within the book itself. I became quite curious about what her book would look like if she had also included her own story, her own reason for being fascinated with this other woman: What was driving her towards Máire Rua? What were the disappointments of her attempt to write this biography?

I think that was very much at the forefront of my mind when I was writing *A Ghost in the Throat*. I really respect my reader (whom I always think about in the singular), and it felt really important to me to create that sense of intimacy with the reader, to open my process and to resist smoothing over the difficulties and the strangeness of attempting a biography.

YFL: And in the process, you immerse the reader in your journey. It's a relationship between you and the reader, isn't it?

DNG: It's so interesting that you say that, because there are certain points within the narrative where I directly address the reader. It was raised to me during the editorial process that this may be a mistake; this may seem too self-conscious, that I might lose the reader's interest by directly addressing them, by breaking the fourth wall.

At the same time, the reader felt so close to me that I felt quite confident in taking that risk. And I think that's part of the reason why readers have responded so warmly to this book; because they feel how closely I'm addressing them.

YFL: Did this journey into Eibhlín Dubh's life as well as your own determine the form the book eventually took?

DNG: Form is something that I'm fascinated by. It's something that challenges me as a reader, something that provokes me and keeps me turning the pages. I love a book that is constructed like a beautifully polished cabinet full of little trapdoors, and I think a lot of readers share my fascination for such challenging books.

As I was writing this book, the working idea I had in my head was that this would be like a book of echoes. My own grounding is in poetry, which I've been writing for most of my writing life. That process would probably be quite familiar to those of us working within the discipline of poetry, to interrogate a poem as it's beginning and to ask how it can reflect some element of its driving force within its form.

Right from the beginning, echoes were so important in trying to communicate the story of my attempt to find out more about the life of Eibhlín Dubh. Echoes are important with the poem itself. And the fact that it is still echoing in our life, that I was investigating her life and sending echoes back to the past; there was this echo back and forth. So I wanted to carry that into the form.

Repetition became very important to me because of that idea of echoes. First of all with the chapters. I tried to mould them so that one chapter would speak from my life in contemporary Ireland, and the next chapter would focus more on Eibhlín

Dubh's life; back and forth like an echo. It was also very important to me that certain phrases within the prose itself would startle the reader by somehow seeming familiar, as they would be repeated throughout the text, back and forth through the chapters as well.

There are many different layers to this book in terms of how I constructed it around echoes, but it was important to do that in a way that was fluid and not draw the reader's attention too much; otherwise it might seem excessive. But it was also really important to me that those echoes were present for the reader. And oftentimes, it's not until the second reading that you'll notice them.

It was playful in a way, to write a book of echoes. That was an element of the book's composition that I really enjoyed. I suppose at an intellectual level, it's like the construction of a puzzle; when you hit on the form that you want to achieve with the book and it's on your mind all the time, and it feels like magic when it comes together.

YFL: Along with the echoing, there also seems to be a sense of writing parallel lives. It was as if you were also interrogating your own life while seeking Eibhlín Dubh's life.

DNG: It's funny when one embarks on this kind of book, one doesn't foresee the kind of revelations about one's own life. I think every book reveals a layer of the self to the writer that was invisible to that point. And it almost happens against our will, like the writing of a book shows you some parts of yourself that you didn't particularly want to dig into, but you can't get away from.

It's something that we rarely speak about as writers, the ways in which our writing can surprise us. Sometimes our writing swerves around; it can be shocking and strange and insists on its own way. Sometimes it doesn't work out the way that we would like it to and it is all the richer because of that, even though it can be very frustrating as it's occurring.

This book led me to some very strange places, and it was a fascinating adventure. I learned a lot about biography, and I learned a lot about myself; about imposter syndrome, which is something I really suffer from. I think this is very evident to anyone who's read the book because I questioned myself explicitly throughout its writing: Who am I to do this? How dare I?

YFL: But your book feels quite personal because you've revealed your vulnerabilities. And you've made Eibhlín Dubh's life more accessible to the reader.

DNG: It's so rewarding to hear that, thank you. I feel a real sense of shared fascination with the life of Eibhlín Dubh Ní Chonaill. My deepest hope for this book is that someone might happen to pick this book up, someone who is much more skilful than I am in research, who will somehow become as fascinated with her life as I am. Someone who will be even more dogged than I was in the pursuit of the historical details. And they will find the answers. I trust that they're out there, I know they are!

YFL: You begin the book with: 'This is a female text'. This phrase is often repeated throughout the book in reference to women's lives, whether yours, Eibhlín Dubh's, even your young daughter's. Could you talk a bit more about this?

DNG: The idea of a female text occurred to me one morning as I visited Kilcrea Abbey, where Eibhlín Dubh Ní Chonaill buried her husband and one of the places where she spoke this extraordinary poem. And as I was driving away, the phrase, 'this is a female text' began to repeat in my head. To begin with, I didn't understand what it meant and I'm not sure that I still fully understand what it means. And I think that's one element of what writing a book is for me; trying to puzzle my way into questions that I don't understand. And that was one of them.

What I found, as I was writing the book, was that I was wondering a lot about how one could define what it is to be a female text, to write a female text, to read a female text. And to what extent can our lives be considered a female text for each individual person? I'm so conscious of how different everybody's life is, and everybody's sense of their own gender and the extent to which that's a force within their own lives. And I'd have huge respect for everybody and the ways in which this feels to them. So this book is just one female text: my attempt to answer the question of what is a female text, using my life as fodder.

The phrase itself became a refrain echoing its way through the book; it recurs as a fresh attempt to answer that question, what is a female text? And as I say, I'm not sure that I still fully have the answer to that question. I have several new answers throughout the writing of the book. But I definitely don't have a definitive answer. It's a subject I'm really curious about, and I'm really interested in reading other people's books and accounts of what it is to consider their lives as a female text and what that means to them, because I suspect that everyone's understanding of that will be different. And some people would reject that idea altogether, which is also fine.

YFL: But with your book, I felt it was a lot about women's invisibility and a reclamation of their voices. Again, there was that parallel of Eibhlín Dubh Ní Chonaill's life in the eighteenth century and yours in the twenty-first century, about how some things may have changed over that time yet there are still some things that stay the same.

DNG: Yeah. And that is always something that astonishes me, when we look towards the past, how much our lives still have in common with people who lived centuries ago, how much of the fabric of our days is similar, but how much is so very, very different.

The ways in which we live our lives now would be unrecognisable to someone who lived in the eighteenth century; the ways in which we think, the ideas that we hold, the music we listen to, the many devices we use. And yet there are elements of our lives now that would still be absolutely recognisable, like the sense of rocking a child to sleep. Small things, like arranging flowers; it's one of the things I can imagine Eibhlín Dubh doing. And as I was writing the book, it felt like everything I did and saw felt somehow connected to her. I think that's familiar to everyone who writes; that sense of when you get deep into a project, everything you see, everything you feel, everything you encounter feels like it's connected; everything chimes with your book. And I really had that sense with this book.

YFL: In the first chapter you talk about inviting the voice of another woman to 'haunt' your throat for a while. By doing so, you are actually giving Eibhlín Dubh a voice, aren't you? This feels significant for someone who was pretty much erased from the historical records you came across in your research.

DNG: It's very upsetting how easily someone's whole life can just be forgotten. A lot of the time I don't think there is intentionality behind that; I don't think women are overlooked or forgotten in the historical records out of spite. If there was active erasure and spitefulness behind it, well, we could just rage at that. But it's even worse that they would be overlooked or forgotten, like they're just seen as being so pointless, not worth looking at.

YFL: You write in such stunning detail, the everyday in women's lives that's often overlooked. I feel that your book centres the domestic – was that your intention?

DNG: It was. As I was considering how women are so often erased and overlooked in historical records, I thought about how they would be doing similar kinds of chores to what I was doing, except I have the benefit of modern machines that really allows me to do so much, like write books as well.

It felt important to me to honour domestic labour. It's so often overlooked, and so little celebrated even by those of us who are engaged in it day in and day out; we don't even acknowledge it ourselves. It was important to me to centre the to-do list that has tasks on it like grocery shopping, mop the floor. They're not grand tasks but they are the kind of labour that keeps families, households together, despite the fact that they're so often overlooked. So it was very important to me to centre that. One of the most radical elements of this book is the fact that the domestic is unapologetically present, and it is celebrated in all its drudgery.

When I was writing and researching for the book, domestic labour was a huge part of my life; it still is. I'm very aware that it isn't the same case for everybody, but it was important for me to be truthful about the shape and the thrust of my days and the fact that so much of it was engaging with domesticity, with the sense that everything keeps heading towards dishevelment and I'm there trying to battle the forces of entropy by just tidying up after toddlers and doing laundry and so on.

YFL: And that never seems to end.

DNG: Never ends, never ends!

YFL: You're a bilingual writer, and the book features your translation of Eibhlín Dubh Ní Chonaill's poem. Tell me a bit more about how important the Irish language is to you.

DNG: I have felt so fortunate all my life to be able to speak the Irish language as well as the English language, because it allows me to access so much of our culture that would be hidden to me otherwise, and so much of our history. Particularly in terms of being able to speak Eibhlín Dubh Ní Chonaill's *Caoineadh Airt Uí Laoghaire* out loud, to feel her voice surging up through my throat and coming to life again, to hear her actual words echoing in the room in the Irish language. It makes me feel so connected to this tradition and to those who came before us. Our language makes me who I am as a person and as a writer. It's such a deep part of my identity.

Also, I think being engaged with one's native language, particularly living in a postcolonial society, allows one to access deep wells of grief and sorrow over all that has been lost. That's something that is very close to the surface for me when I speak in Irish and when I communicate with others who speak Irish. It's only a minority of people in Ireland who speak fluent Irish now.

YFL: It comes through in the book as well, the essence of the language, the connection.

DNG: Engaging with the Irish language for me is definitely a way of seeking connection with others and with readers too. And it's wonderful to me that anyone who picks up this book isn't just picking up the story of this adventure to find out more about Eibhlín Dubh Ní Chonaill's life. They're also picking up her Caoineadh, which is published in full at the back of the book; her words in the Irish language are part of the very fabric of the book. And so it feels like her presence is embedded in this book in a very true way.

YFL: You've given her that space for her voice to soar.

DNG: I hope so. It feels like an important part of my life's work, to honour her life. It has been such a gift to me in my own life, this relationship with Eibhlín Dubh, and the admiration that is always growing within me for her, and for her life.

YFL: *A Ghost in the Throat* is your first work of prose. Has it inspired you to write more?

DNG: I've just begun my next book of prose. It's very, very early days. When I begin a new book it's a little like entering a dark room and feeling around on the walls for the light switch. So I haven't found the light switch. I don't know what it is I'm aiming to write. But I'm really enjoying walking around in the darkness, feeling blindly for the light switch.

A Ghost in The Throat *is out in paperback from Tramp Press* **H**

Like what you've read?

Sign up for a subscription and get our next batch of stand-out writing delivered direct to your door, desktop or tablet.

Annual print & digital subscription £40
Four issues, p&p free

Annual digital subscription £20
Four issues, saving £4 off list price

Subscribers also enjoy the benefit of being able to submit their writing to Hinterland free of charge.

Visit our website to subscribe:

www.hinterlandnonfiction.com/subscribe